THIRST

ALICE OWENS JOHNSON

outskirts
press

Dedication

Eulalie McKay Johnson
Shelby Flowers Ferris
Best Friends for Life

ACKNOWLEDGMENT

I wish to thank my former teachers who have encouraged me and helped me over the years:

Cathy Smith Bowers Joseph Bathanti, Gayle Adams, Abigail Dewitt, Tommy Hayes, Michael Parker, Fred Chapell

Ann Deagon, Sebastian Matthews, Kevin McIlvoy, Rebecca McClanahan, Rosemary Daniel, John Dufresnen,

Robin Hemly, Marjorie Hudson, Virginia McCullough, Peggy Millin. Also, to my fellow writers in workshops and critique groups over the years. Special Thanks to my best reader, my husband of 55 years Lee McKay Johnson.

PART I

THIRST

OUR JOURNEY BEGAN in 1968 in Morocco on Spring break. We'd been living in Paris, but the student riots were making life impossible. We had dodged confrontations between students and police, navigated through burning automobiles and lived in a world without news. DeGaulle had cut off the public radio and inserted swing music, an odd score to the sounds of bombs going off on nearby roofs. And so we decided to borrow a friend's VW bug, pile myself, my husband, brother-in-law and friend Bob inside. From the outside, we looked like the opening act in a circus.

Morocco was the most exotic country we'd ever seen. It wasn't just the high Atlas Mountains, the desert oasis, or the ubiquitous date palms, it was the architecture. Outside of Rome, Fez was the most ancient city I'd ever visited. As we drove closer to the city, we could make out the mud palaces with gigantic doors; but we could never have imagined what life teemed within the walls. Before we got to the souks, we'd passed acrobats and snake charmers outside the gates.

Fez's enormous wooden gates resembled the passage through which the Trojan horse might have entered. Instantly we were assaulted with sights, sounds and smells dazzling our senses as we traveled through a street only wide enough to accommodate our VW bug. Rich aromas assaulted us: cinnamon, cardamom, paprika, turmeric, cumin, fenugreek all stuffed in bags blazing in color. Donkeys laden with lamb and goat carcasses brushed past our car, smothered in flies. Berber rugs, waterfalls of them, cascaded from high windows, vats of olives, ceramics, metal works announced a culture where arts were celebrated. I was dazzled as my stomach churned from the overwhelming smells.

Men shook their fists at us, our first hint we weren't driving on an actual street, as we nosed through the souks. I kept seeing odd stalls and dark shops with snakes, monkeys, turtles and birds. Where had we landed?

Once out of the market, the *medina,* we began to see the amazing buildings, palaces constructed of mud, arches, colonnades. Half-closed doors let us peek into courtyards heavy with fruit trees, honeysuckle, and fountains slapping. We'd stepped out of time into fantasy. Morocco, a country contrasts. From the street most homes were stark blocks of dirt but once inside it was all color, carving, artistry and olfactory overload: courtyards stuffed with mint, geranium, basil, jasmine. I often saw bowls of water with floating rose petals, the kind of soft celebration that made a girl like me want to ululate with joy.

Wherever we traveled in Morocco we were given a new visual gift but the most overwhelming, over and over, was the architecture, mud castles as much as four hundred years old, Arab, North African, the Orient all blended into a woven dream. I was constantly running my hands over the plastered walls of the buildings textured and inviting. The streets were mazes of buildings with arched doorways, stained glass, mosaics and stucco moldings. The massive doors to these homes had hinges the size of a television sets. I kept exchanging looks with my husband Lee. We were sunk, hooked, plunged into this fantasy world of the Arabian Nights.

In Marrakech I remembered seeing barbers against the city walls, cutting hair. Barbers served other purposes too, such as dentistry and most likely circumcision (Muslims are all circumcised). It was a place of danger even back then. One of the first things I did when we got to a hotel was to take out a scarf, cover my head and let my hems down on the one skirt I had for traveling. It wasn't a burka, but it was better than my mini length which drew stares from men and women. As we spoke French, we weren't being pegged as Americans. During the Viet Nam era, we had learned to be careful about identifying our nationality abroad.

One afternoon a man in a jellaba warned me, in French, to stay inside on Thursdays. When I asked why he said Thursdays were the days when the white slavers came to the medina. They especially liked blondes. Like me. Oh. I see.

When we left Fez for the desert oasis of Ourzazate, we took something as Rocky as a goat path through the High Atlas Mountains. We were stopped continuously by young boys thrusting chipmunks dangling by ropes. I didn't know if they were supposed to be pets or dinner. If that ploy didn't get us to buy something, they held up gigantic pieces of quartz crystal with amethyst glittering in the hot mountain sun.

It was a rough journey also because we were headed for the only hotel in Ourzazate and some Frenchmen kept trying to run us off the road to get to that one room.

There is no passing lane on such a narrow road. But we got there, secured a room then collapsed. When the man at the desk suggested we go to a specific eatery because there was a good chance the local pasha might show for dinner, we signed on.

That evening we went walking into one of the largest courtyards I'd ever seen.

It was perhaps fifty feet high, with one balcony for eating and a mezzanine where tables were set with white cloths. About halfway through our meal we heard the low thud of what sounded like an oncoming train.

As the sounds got closer, it was clear to us we'd heard the beckoning call of drums. Through the double doors forty drummers emerged beating enormous drums, followed by women scarved and beaded, gyrating, spinning and ululating. Then the evening began and began and began. The arrival of the pasha set the women into more frenetic dancing. Our trance was complete.

1970 was a year like the dust bowl depression for Ph.D. candidates in English.

At the MLA convention Lee attended earlier that spring, he said people had made badges announcing their specialty. My favorite was a huge BLAKE ANYONE?

It seemed like the best way to sell yourself at the MLA was with something akin to a sandwich board.

We left California in the Spring and drove across the U.S.A., son Morgan strapped into the back seat like a papoose. Morgan was restless and tired from being penned in for so many hours a day and I was exhausted from being pregnant and not getting enough exercise myself. But we pushed on like pioneers as we targeted three schools where Lee might find a job. Our initial visit to New Mexico was disorienting. I gaped at the Sandia Mountain range, punched out of a khaki-colored landscape, a granite fist, the entire horizon nearly bereft of trees and foliage. I've never really been fond of cactus. They are not exactly warm and fuzzy plants, and most of the yards around the University of New Mexico were filled with white rocks, the kind I associated with the bottoms of aquariums. The air was so dry, I nearly got nose bleeds and continually swathed my nostrils with tiny dabs of Vaseline. We had targeted three schools, U.N.M, Vermont's myriad of small schools and a few interesting spots in Florida. Then we drove home, back to the swamps.

We finally crossed the Mississippi again, smelling the brackish Louisiana air. Home: New Orleans where we waited for a letter from one of the schools. It was like watching election returns. And It wasn't until New Orleans I had a proper visit to the OB-Gyn from whom I learned I slightly miscalculated the birth of our new baby. I'd been nursing Morgan, so I never had any period for over a year, which made calculating the arrival date difficult. Best we could figure it would be the end of September. In late Spring, we got the news from U.N.M. and began packing, me saying goodbye to magnolias, gardenias, night-blooming jasmine and palm trees. As we drove back across the country, we began to think about our new home state, recalling a short drive through the old town of Santa Fe, with its shady lanes and adobe homes. New Orleans is a gauntlet to any city in the world. We would have to find our connection to a place that could not have been a greater contrast to New Orleans. And, Lee reminded me, we weren't going to be living in Santa Fe, we'd be in Albuquerque. Wherever we landed, we'd have to create our atmosphere. And so we began to fantasize about adobe houses. It was a way to get through Texas.

After driving around with an Albuquerque realtor through the University section of town, we knew we had to find a place, a setting, more exotic.

"I can't live in a stucco house," I said after an exhausting day with Morgan bouncing around the back seat. "And after having an exuberant child in her car all day, I don't think that realtor really wants to deal with us again." Morgan loved to make car noises like brmm brmmm continually. It worried me we might have spawned a race car driver. "Better than a truck driver," Lee said. We learned to live with it like white noise.

We chose a rental house in Corrales we'd found in the paper, about twenty miles out of town. Although it wasn't a real adobe, it had the feel of an adobe, it even had a small screen porch where we often slept. Our furniture seemed to have been parked somewhere near Tucumcari, but they promised it would be in our area soon.

The days were blazing hot, the nights sweet and cool. Cottonwoods surrounded our faux adobe, the leaves bright green. Each night we took a walk alongside the ditch while Morgan ran down the corduroy road. The heavy summer rains were over.

I remember the dirt road we walked looking almost purple in the late afternoon light, Morgan's long shadows as he sprinted ahead of us. It was a sweet place with Hispanic families dotting the ditch road, the acequias, ditches, ran along the length of the field for irrigation. Horses and other cloven animals surrounded us. The smell of alfalfa and hay permeated the air. Periodically between the sounds of crowing roosters, we heard the happy oinks of a pig family. Land in New Mexico, we learned by walking it, was carved into long pieces. We were told they were owned by families who left room for the next generation, placing the elders at the end of the lot, the offspring towards the noisy main road. In New Orleans family crypts are stacked up on one another like ovens. Real estate is high in the best cemeteries and the word was that the coffins rotted and crashed to the lower floor making room for the latest member of the family.

We became friendly with the Armijo family: Rudy, Dixie, and Johnny.

My first objective when I got to our new home was to find a good doctor for me and a pediatrician for Morgan. We needed to get ready for our new baby, and get oriented in a city cut into grids, so different from the winding streets in New Orleans where streets obeyed the bends in the Mississippi River. We didn't know a soul. Lee's grandmother had given us the names of an elderly couple she vaguely knew who had lived in her hometown Vicksburg, Mississippi.

We also worked together to build an adobe house. Each evening we strolled down the corrugated road, the calling card of New Mexico. We chatted with them and watched the family effort: laying one brick on another. In a month the walls were waist high with everyone at the task, loading dirt into a cement mixer for mortar, troweling the mud, handing bricks in a fire line. It seemed so efficient. Their walls were one adobe thick, about twelve inches. Neither of us said anything about building until their windows went up, then the door frames in place. We'd watched the zygote reach maturity. Over and over we said to one another, "It looks so easy."

Without any radio, or television, we often used our long afternoons noodling around with house ideas. All the building around us had a buzzing contagious feel to it. Territorial style, we decided, was reminiscent of southern homes with high ceilings and wide portals. It was so dry in this new climate, we realized we could use a shaded portal for months longer than a Southern front porch, without fear of the dreaded mildew.

One bright early August day I woke up feeling peppy, something I had missed for the last eight months. I took the car to do a little exploring while Lee stayed with Morgan. I drove down Fourth Street taking note of little hide-away places I'd like to explore in the future, enjoying the feeling of being in a new place, noticing the old adobe homes, some crumbling, in the north valley. One store in particular caught my attention. An adobe building probably fifty years old set back off the road, making it easy to pull in. There were old doors, knick-knacks and things we didn't need luring me in. I loved the painted blue windows of the little *bottega,* the geraniums out front. I strolled in, toyed with interesting things I never saw in the South: ancient tortilla presses, saddles, horse blankets. I found a neat pair of spurs I could twirl and was hoping to find Marshall Dillon's badge in a box of snarled metal objects. I picked up what looked like two bent coat hangers. "What's this?" I asked. The owner replied, "Dowsing rods."

For the first time I realized I'd really arrived on foreign turf. Where I came from I could hit water in my own back yard with a big serving spoon. The owner was messing about with an old clock as I bumped along the aisles, my big baby belly nearly knocking over a beautiful wooden dough bowl. He let me peruse at my leisure, but finally asked. "Anything special you looking for?

Before I could formulate the thought, the words jumped out of my mouth. "Yes, I'm looking for a stained-glass window for my daughter's room. We're building our own adobe."

"How old is your daughter?" He asked guiding me to the perfect stained glass window propped up in the back of the store. Instead of answering him, I pointed to my big belly.

He looked up in surprise. "How do you know it's a girl?

"She just told me." And I bought the window.

All the way home I glanced in the back seat of the car wondering how on earth I would explain what had just happened. The colors in the newly purchased window were soft pastels, blues, lavenders. was triangular in shape and had something sacred about it I couldn't name. I tried to puzzle out this odd purchase, the certain knowledge we were about to have a daughter and the very perplexing words that had come out of my mouth the astonishing fact that we'd be building our own house. We'd only talked about this building plan a few times, thinking about it as a dream far away, even though we'd drawn fantasy houses. But in the next week I went into labor. And by midyear we'd bought our land on the mesa.

The long drive to the grocery in Corrales gave me time to breathe. I thought about our journey, the book of Mormon I'd discovered in the motel where I usually found a bible. As I perused the earth, the "dirt" looked like corn flower or tortillas. Sometimes I started thinking I'd step over the edge of sanity and float above the Sandias like the giant balloons I'd seen wafting by.

As I drove back to our "home" I noticed that down by the river I saw that the banks were piled up mud flats, no levee like Louisiana. The Rio Grande was neither. I was fairly certain there were crocodiles or alligators lurking in the mire. This was not the land of milk and honey. The women I'd seen in the grocery had saddle bag complexions. I could not guess their ages. Lee had told me the banks of the river had exotic trees? Really? The first thing I said as I stormed through our door was There are no trees!"

"Calm down. It's just the pregnancy making you feel so nuts."

"I'm nuts? They aren't even Christians here—that drawer in the hotel had The Book of Mormon in it, not a vestige of the bible." I sat down in the coolest corner of the house wondering what in the world I'd been talked in.

A few days later I went into labor. At first, I thought it was the chile I'd eaten, but around two a.m. it became abundantly clear this baby was coming.

"Now what? What do we do about Morgan? I don't know anyone here. I can't call that nice woman across the ditch. She's about to have a baby herself." I looked out the window at the full moon on the mesas, the sky a thicket of stars. "What about that old couple, the friends Mimi told us about," Lee said. "The ones from Vicksburg?"

"Didn't she tell us they were elderly?"

"Any other ideas?' So we called the Simms family at four am.

"Hi," Lee began. "This is Lee Johnson. My grandmother Mary Mckay gave us your name. We just moved here from Orleans."

I listened in as she responded in her thick Mississippi drawl.

There was a groggy pause from Donald and Sarah's phone. "Well, Mary Mckay's grandson, well."

Lee added quickly, "We're having a baby."

"Isn't that lovely. Honey, do you know what time it is?"

"No, please listen. We're having it right now. My wife is in labor."

"Do you want the name of a doctor?"

Then he explained the situation to them. There was such a deep silence, I quit counting the minutes between contractions wondering what they might be thinking about Lee's plea to watch our lovely toddler who we *tried* to pass off as sedate.

As dawn rose, we drove into their neighborhood, getting lost in the grid system of houses all looking alike. Sarah was standing at the door in a house coat. We opened the door and Morgan darted out like a cat out of a cage. Lee ran after him yelling, "That's Morgan."

I saw the old woman put her hand to her jaw. "Oh, my."

The elderly Donald walked with a cane. "I'll be fine, have had lots of youngsters in my time," he reassured us in a tone half jovial and half annoyed. I looked into the rear-view mirror watching poor Donald trying to corral Morgan into their home which I was certain was filled with doo daws and little glass figurines.

At the hospital, B.C.M.C., I thought I could relax and lie down, but the attendant, a fellow with a white turban wrapped around his head, told me in broken terms that sounded like a diagrammed sentence, I probably wasn't in labor and I'd have to come back as the hospital was filled. I looked despairingly at the crowded corridor filled with Hispanics and Indians.

And so I spent the next five centimeters in the Rexall Drug store across the street, panting in a plastic red leatherette booth in freezing air conditioning while a waitress tried to persuade me not to have that baby in her "station." I had no time to consider our new baby when I was finally admitted. In fact, Lilah's debut was one of the scariest moments of my life. I heard the monitor drop, saw the man in the turban turn the color of parchment, then he called for a stretcher and we began a roller derby down the hall to delivery. The heavy nurses practically threw me on the table.

"Put your feet in those stirrups and push as if your life depends on it." When I put my feet in the stirrups, the metal feet holders crashed to the floor. "Now what?"

"Grab your ankles," she shouted as the bright lights blared in my face, Lee about to faint. Then, just to make sure Lilah made it through the birth canal, her heart beat falling, the nurse, who weighed in at about 190 began pushing on my belly, all the while the magnified heartbeat dropping, in a moment of panic the nurse thrust her body across mine, pushing my daughter as if coaxing a cow out of pen. "Push like your life depended on it," she said. With all the chaos and coaching, Lilah's birth was silent, too silent. Then she let loose with her hallmark cry, our little lion daughter. She was alive, announcing her place on the planet, a citizen of New Mexico.

Even on one day one I could see Lilah would make her way in the world with fierce determination. Her great-great grandmother was part Choctaw and single handedly ran a timber operation after the Civil War outside of Meridian, Mississippi. Lilah's brow was already furrowed. History was shining back at me so clearly I could practically hear paddle wheel boats and calliope music. Was I just a vehicle for this little leonine baby?

Staying in the county hospital birth ward was no soiree. I was the only mother in there nursing. Somehow all these Spanish women were given small prepared bottles, keeping the babies being on a timetable for feeding. The nurse's timetable. Since I was the only annoying mother who thought breasts were made for giving milk, I was told I would have to get up, go to the nursery and feed Lilah myself. The woman next to me, Valdez, her name written on the bed, shrugged. Planned Parenthood, or an organization like them, spent a good hour trying to persuade Valdez to have her tubes tied. But she was adamant, even though this was her ninth child. So far, I'd seen three different men come in and smile proudly, talk about how much this baby boy resembled his side of the family.

I couldn't figure out how to get out of this nightmare with my newborn. But the fun wasn't over yet. A thug, disguised as a nurse, came up to my bedside. "No seeing the baby until you've had a sitz bath. Hospital rules."

Where was I? Pakistan? When we got to the aluminum tub she said, "And when you're done, you have to clean out the tub." She showed me a bottle of antiseptic, then left me to drown. In a few minutes she returned. "Ain't going to faint, are you?"

"Nope. Wouldn't give you that satisfaction." I decided I was first going to something then somehow get out of this place.

Mealtime came rumbling in on aluminum trays. A blue plastic lid covered the first thing I'd had to eat in over thirty hours. I lifted the top: hot dogs and chile. I was on the verge of throwing the dish against the disturbingly dirty green wall when Valdez intervened. "Hey, Johnson. You not going to eat that?"

"Not if you paid me." "Then let me have it."

I leaned towards her tipping over the Styrofoam cup, the water splooshing all over the floor. I could hear Valdez munching down the meal and tried not to think of what punishment the nurses would dream up for me for turning over the water.

There was no sleeping in this postpartum dorm. Between the sound of babies sucking on bottles, balloons rubbing together and Laundromat chitchat from bed to bed I was on the verge of some sort of Nazi sleep-deprived break down. To make things worse, the nurses told me Lilah's crying was causing a riot in the nursery. What mother can sleep with the plaintiff cry of a baby unattended? I was leaving, going home as soon as I could check out. And I did, Lilah in my arms and

Morgan pushing the wheelchairs in the lobby into new places.

The next morning, I convinced them I could get along at home. And I did. Our old soul baby was a non-sleeper. The only thing which seemed to lull her was a ride in the car, and so we'd drive on the endless stretches of road leading towards Taos was because of these forays we began to see the extreme frozen music of the landscape, watch the blue haze over the Jemez mountains and see the pentimento of the earth's crust reveal itself. Lilah was about two weeks old when we first saw the zome at Lama Foundation near Taos. It beckoned from miles away. There was nothing as tall except the mountain range behind it. We'd been driving around toying with different design ideas about a fantasy house. It must have been that drive when the tricksters threw us underneath the wheels of reality. We stopped, drove up to it, then boldly entered a building probably forty feet high. The octagonal building roofed with interconnected panels, a pointed dome reaching for the sky. It was a zome.

Domes were interesting, but this structure had a different kind of integrity. We had walked into the heart of something that was related to a family of shapes: pinecones, pineapples, natural things so woven they produced a feeling of unity. That inexplicable oneness zonked the two of us simultaneously. When we exchanged glances we were both wearing goofy grins like a person getting stoned for the first time. This soaring structure produced something like a natural high. "This is like stepping into an artichoke," I whispered to Lee. "A honeycomb," he whispered back. "A crystal." I raised him one. With each jump our awe echoed around the structure, a sacred cave. We were sunk, dazzled with a structure that replicated the DNA within us. "Oh, Lordy," I said. "I really want this." He squeezed my hand.

Lama Foundation's statement of purpose was to awaken consciousness through harmonious development. Even though we'd lived in the depths of the flower children culture in California, this building had an edge to it that bypassed the cliché of peace and love. I didn't know much about Zen, yet. I knew when I stepped inside the zome, I'd crossed a large threshold. We were sealed into our destiny and somewhere the gods were kicking back and having a good laugh, switching their channels to the latest sit-com: The Johnson show.

I'm not sure what clicked as we drove home, but we clearly were headed down a new road. One of the most frequently asked questions at the chamber of commerce in Albuquerque was *Is it necessary to have a passport to go there?* For some odd reason birthing a child in New Mexico, a land of exotic extremes made us feel more part of this world. Three weeks later we decided to take the plunge and buy land. Build our own house. Our work, our design. No architect needed. We were certifiable crazy.

First the land: a piece on a mesa thirty minutes from Albuquerque outside a village called Placitas. The first owners of the land were Native Indians from the Santa Ana Pueblo. I discovered pottery shards the first time we stood looking one hundred miles ahead towards the mesas at an inactive volcano named *Cabezon.* Indian lore had it that *Cabezon* was the decapitated head of a larger mountain eighty miles to the west called Mount Taylor. We'd happily slipped into the world of folk lore and mythology.

Behind us the *Sandia* Mountains loomed craggy and defiant. At sunset they blushed the color of watermelon. Our land was spell- binding. And so we began to construct our crazy dream.

Morocco still had us in its grips. This mesmerizing place changed our consciousness, invited us into the world of kasbahs and mud palaces, exotic tiled rooms, harsh climate and deep interiors. The tactile allure of the buildings in Fez had invited us to explore the possibility of living in a home that felt like a thrown pot. We were both dizzy with our visions of mud compounds, gigantic walls with gates wide enough to allow a dozen loping camels inside. We needed to snap out of our dream, but we didn't. And now that we lived in New Mexico the fantasy of living inside the thick interior of mud walls continually nipped at our minds until we gave into our whimsy. Now we conceived of a fantasy architectural type we dubbed, Moroccan adobe. It was the zome that lured us deeper into our dream illusion. We could live in something that felt like a mosque. We wouldn't have to get enlightened, we'd build enlightened.

The alluring addiction to design and building houses is still the bedrock of our forty-five year marriage. People told us right from the start we might build our home, but we'd never stay married. Somehow, we survived. We found the land.

Building our home in New Mexico with our own two hands probably wasn't a very smart idea. Neither Lee nor I had any experience.
As my father said, "Lee can't even hang a towel rack." He banged the
table like Kruschev with his shoe. "You are both crazy, hair-brained
hippies." We were branded as dreamers, thoroughly irresponsible. Yep,
that seemed to be our marriage of weaknesses. At the time we were only
married five years. I thought perhaps building dream castles wasn't
such a bad addiction, like gambling. And I thought perhaps we'd do it
once and get the thrill and risk of such a venture out of our system. But
now, each time we sit down with a piece of paper and two pencils our
designs begin to fly. We are now married for forty-five years. I realized
we were hopelessly tied to creating spaces, realizing pipe dreams. As a
friend told me, "you are totally delusional."

"Good, then," I replied to this insult. "I hate doing anything
half-assed."

There was something magical and contagious about this part of the
world in the 1970's. Once we both saw the magic of the Southwest, it
was as if we'd signed a contract. Lenses changed and we were given the
vision to see clearly the deep wonder of the desert. We used the code
word "magic" between us, as it seemed we really hadn't been attuned
to the full beauty of the surroundings, then bingo, we saw the figure
in the carpet, as Henry James called it. It had been sitting patiently
before us, but it took a fanciful structure like the zome at Lama to give
it a centering point. Then the backdrop revealed itself and we were
instantly in Oz, that magical moment when the film suddenly flipped
from black and white into blazing Mannerist color. What had been
beige, khaki and faded intensified into purple, red, brown and watermelon pink at sunset.

We began to share our building dream with people we met, just
to test out the crazy factor. Nobody out there seemed to be surprised,
even when we threw in, we'd never done anything like this. One reply
stuck in my mind: "Looks like New Mexico has chosen you." Once we
knew we were going ahead with crazy scheme, we sought advice only
from those who would support us, avoiding the tongue clucking of say
Lee's colleagues at the University.

Our land was a tract owned by the Bureau of Land Management.
The owners who lived in a trailer park in the village, bought it from

the BLM. When we went to sign the papers, a woman looking like a German hausfrau opened the door. Her pale hair was slicked into a bun and her eyes were sparkly bright. She wore a man's wrinkled tuxedo shirt and a Kotex belt. Her husband lumbered into the room. She pointed to him. "That's my man. I just had his nuts cut off." She laughed and smacked his bottom.

I had deep thoughts about the legitimacy of this deal. How could legitimate people shuffle around the desert in nothing but Kotex belt? I didn't disbelieve her "joke" about having his 'nuts cut off. Rather than hear the details of his vasectomy, we signed the papers and left.

"Welcome to Placitas," I told Lee.

"What have we just done?"

That afternoon we drove the rugged road onto our land with Lilah swaddled down and Morgan straining to get out of the car. When I pivoted to the right I could make out the snow caps of the Sangre de Cristo Mountains of Santa Fe. The scale of life out there was preposterous: hills dotted with juniper bushes darkened at sunset. I felt I was standing next to tiny sponge trees glued to my brother's model railroad train table. I'd never seen so much nothing.

As we drove, Lee related the history, if you could call it that, of the land. The Santa Ana Indians had inhabited our land, originally using it for grazing, then migrated to the richer soil of the Rio Grande Valley below. I can't understand what cattle might have grazed on, and I liked to think there was once a forest where now there was nothing but junipers, chamisa, cactus and occasional hub caps and beer cans. This land was untillable.

Our piece of the world gave the phrase "miles from nowhere" new meaning. At first, I could only see bright white light, and then my eyes learned to discern from wavy heat images to well-defined mountain ranges. From our perch we could see the bright green line of cottonwood trees in Bernallilo about ten miles away, the Rio Grande snaking through the crusty land. The *bosque,* the land around the Rio Grande, was an oasis, bright green with waving cottonwoods roots deep in rich brown earth. Beyond that were miles, nearly eighty, of mesas and arroyos, the hazy blue Jemez mountains, the extinct volcano, *Cabezon,* and on the other side of the highway, the Placitas town dump. The planet had lifted its skirt, showed us the underside of a new world we wanted.

We were the first inhabitants, pioneers with the old Eleanor Roosevelt spirit of being able to do anything we set our minds to. The Indians used the land for pasture, we were told. On the first day we were there I discovered a little piece of pottery that felt like a piece of good luck.

It would be our task to honor this land, keep everything close to nature with underground phone and utility lines. As there was no road, we simply drove over the hard-packed earth trying different curves and straightaways until we had the most direct route to our piece of the property. We didn't know at the time, we'd actually set a course on the map by carving out this circuit. And as for building low, as in kasbahs, everything had changed when we saw the "zome" at the Lama Foundation in Taos. We wanted to incorporate Morocco, Mexico and this new structure, this zome, and weave it together honoring all we loved.

When we found the piece of our planet that was now ours, we understood our eyes would have to learn to see more than they'd ever seen. This unfettered world would come into focus daily until we could identify life on a manageable scale. I used to play a game as a child having to do with hidden figures in a landscape. On first glance I couldn't find the cat, or the pipe, or the drum in the picture, but then my eyes caught a shape, and the odd out of place item grew clearer. That's how it was looking at the mesas, the volcano, the mountains. It seemed to me early on the gods liked playing games with us mortals. Tricksters were part of the Indian culture we stood on; add to that the Merry Prankster effect of the nomad hippies who moved in large numbers from California to New Mexico. Add to that the superstitions of the Hispanic people, descended from Spain in a culture loaded with myth and secrecy. And of course, the West abounds with Wiley Coyote and roadrunner stories, in the same canon as Paul Bunyan. Voila, the cultures swirled around us like gremlin soup. Sometimes we saw the world and sometimes we missed it entirely. Sometimes I didn't want to see. So many gods and demons at play. Could we take this harsh challenge on?

We were on a straight course to the hidden passage that connects the mind with full-blown fantasy. The universe helped us out. To our delight, the designer of the zome, Steve Baer, lived in Corrales a few ditches away from our rented home. Coincidence?

That first night after seeing the zome at Lama Foundation, before our dreams started to find shape and fancy, we sat there transfixed until the night sagged with stars.

First you dig the well. Drill through layers of the earth's crust until you think you've hit molten magma. Each foot more and more costly as the bit finally strikes it rich: water.

Going through a third of our money just to get the water was shocking. Our determination was fierce. Our ignorance stellar.

For months we drew pictures of how we wanted our house to look, ripping through tablets of paper, changing diapers and keeping track of our active son who moved with the alacrity of a jack rabbit. Lee was teaching at the University and I was trying to stay sane with a newborn and a toddler who climbed before he crawled. I discovered his climbing skills when he scaled a dresser getting hold of a bottle of cough medicine and drinking the entire thing. This took us to the emergency room where he was given Ipecac producing something like projectile vomiting. In another instance he managed to climb up onto a shelf where I stored our five-gallon jar of honey. Not only did he unscrew the lid, he dripped honey all over himself, then left a sticky trail throughout our house.

And so our home began to take shape on paper with a twenty two foot zome as a living room, adobe arms wrapping around it, walls that curved, dipped and climbed to twelve feet.

Architecturally we went for something extravagant: a 72-foot axis through the center of the house where we could look through four arches. At one end was the fireplace in the kitchen, at the other end the fire place in the zome. When we had parties, we lit fires in both.

Our dream had no limit, our wallet did. We wanted the feel of a hacienda nudged up next to a mosque. With adobe, all of these possibilities existed. We met with Steve to talk about our dream house with a zome as its main focus.

Steve is an intense guy, he was known throughout the West for his innovative ideas, having worked with "Bucky" Fuller and other famous folk who strayed through the ever-changing idea of what a home should be. Steve told us we needed to choose a magic number for our building. We liked that. We picked 22. I can't recall if we opened the *I Ching*, threw some coins and let it decide our fate. We often did that. I'm thinking we came to this number because we liked it. Lee had a penchant for nines, I personally loved threes, but was also partial to eights, so we picked twenty-two.

The zome: twenty-two feet high, twenty-two feet across. We returned to Steve's place of business in Albuquerque, Zomeworks. Before the ink on our contract was dry Steve gave us a warning. "Every measurement in that space has to be exact so the panels fit in perfectly. The walls must be *absolutely* straight, no wobbly stuff." Scary.

Steve's eyes were so intense they practically sparked blue flames. And so Steve came to our land to transit the zome. A feeling of well-being settled around us. He was in charge of the math. Then we learned the exciting fact that the roof panels of the zome were erected in one day, almost like living in a trailer, we thought. Steve had a timetable. We had just stepped across the line, ready or not.

We had a sense of false security knowing Steve was taking care of the center of our home, but the rest, the adobe arms around the zome, kitchen, bedrooms and baths were up to us. Because we'd both grown up in New Orleans, we had a penchant for tall ceilings, large windows, and spaciousness. What had crept into our architectural floor plan was the use of adobe, the possibility of actually sculpting the interior and the exterior any way we wanted. Our thick wall fantasy sprang to life as we saw the possibilities of rounded walls, portals reminiscent of Egypt and places like Santa Fe. The windows facing the mesa would be in the territorial style, but the rest was going to be something like Mexican/territorial/Moroccan. We made a commitment right from the start, we'd use only one adobe on the walls of the zome, but the rest of the house would be two adobes thick, that is to say twenty four inches thick, a fortress. We didn't even consider we could have built two houses with that many bricks. It was an understatement to say we didn't have a full scope on the scale of things.

I remember walking out on the land before Steve did his sightings. We wanted the house tilted towards the south for the solar effect. Steve had a theory that if your insulation is good, you can heat your house with a candle. I loved his thinking. No one I knew in the world of architecture had a mind like Steve's. But I'm glad he didn't arrive to see how we were coming at our own calculations.

There were many benefits from befriending Steve and his wife Holly. They were selling their beautiful adobe home down the ditch from us when we rented a place in Corrales; building a house on the mesa completely made of aluminum. The south facing wall of their home was hand-cranked open each day and stacked barrels of water warmed the house. At night they cranked up the walls, called "skylids."

Holly told me her heritage was Swiss and so I imagined them at sunset lowering the skylids in Swiss cuckoo clock fashion. It was exciting to see people with that much ingenuity and belief in their invention. I don't think I ever saw Steve without a thermometer on him, like some kind of geothermal gun slinger.

Outside their aluminum wonder, a huge windmill creaked power and water all generated by nature. They were the first people I knew who honestly lived off the grid. And Steve's creativity was a magnet to all sorts of interesting folk. Once we passed a visitor to their house driving a black limo with long steer great horns strapped to the bumper. This man turned out to be Stanley Marsh, an eccentric millionaire from the Texas pan handle who'd constructed a "Cadillac ranch" in Amarillo by burying a fleet of old Cadillacs into the ground, nose down, tails up. We'd actually passed his odd installation once, it looked like a monument created by aliens. All of the cars faced West as if they were an odd cult. When we first saw it, we referred to it as a metallic Stone Henge. But that wasn't the end of his odd monuments. Later, Stanley also erected something he called "The Floating Mesa," an environmental sculpture that spanned the earth with a giant canvas. He wanted to construct something that made the mesa appear to be suspended in the sky. I didn't need an artificial piece of art to make me feel suspended. When I looked into the ghostly world of the mesas, I was already sailing in an odd sea.

Because the scale of the world on our spit of land was so huge, we decided to bring out some props and have a *faux* dinner party, trying to guess how large the kitchen might be, the spaces in between. And so we placed chairs out on the desolate mesa and tried a civil conversation, continually moving the chairs in closer as we calculated how large a room needed to be for the right ambience, the repartee.

"Pass the wine, please," I yelled to Lee.

"What?"

The wind blew our voices in the wrong direction. "I said this bison's a bit over cooked."

"No jello?" Lee said. "I love it when you make that jiggly desert that looks like a brain."

Just then a dirt dervish appeared as an unwanted guest. Our entire make-believe method had to be abandoned, our imaginary guests leaving in a huff.

When we traveled in Europe in 1968 we got into the habit of pacing off rooms that left us feeling elevated, inspired. This habit got us into trouble in the Sir John Soames house in London as Lee walked past the cordoned off area counting the feet, trying to guess the perimeters we'd both admired. We had the habit of stopping in our tracks when we'd come across a perfectly balanced room. At this mutual admiration point, one of us would take out paper and pen while the other began heel-to-toe measuring. In this historically beautiful London museum, the guard took the two of us aside, behind muffled curtains, and began questioning our motives. Terrorism in the U.S. was relatively unknown, but everyone in England feared the IRA. Innocents abroad.

It was much easier to figure out the harmony of a built room then the wide-open spaces of our newly acquired land. Our reckonings on the desert floor turned out to be slightly on the absurd side. We were without any natural perimeters most people in more civilized settings use, such things as trees, boxwood hedges, and so on, to determine their room sizes. But as we were in the throne room of the great Buddah, we couldn't gauge the size of anything. Instead, we went at our project with a measuring tape visiting impressive already constructed adobes homes, their already built rooms as a guideline for our house. We carried notebooks with descriptions of rooms that had an ambience we liked, the old ones in Corrales, Santa Fe and all places in between. Not only did we visit some beautiful old haciendas, but we got to hear their building stories.

One house owned by a Dr. Menge, on the back road of Corrales had fabulous proportions, courtyards and an extra added element, the walls were painted in mud from places all over New Mexico: yellow mud, even purple mud and one room was white mud and sparkled with mica. But the most spectacular hill was called LaBajada. We were enchanted with the idea of wrapping the walls in the zome with this color. And so we added to our tasks the toting of bags and bags of this mud back to our site. It was a royal color that deepened according to the sun. But first all the mud had to go through a sieve, then mixed with water and finally hand mud plastered onto the zome walls. We were ready for royalty.

Our house was shaping up with real statistics. But money, already, was slipping through our fingers like *masa*.

Another thing changed from the visit to the Menge house when we stepped onto his wide portal, the equivalent of a verandah. His portal was wide enough for dining tables and chairs. It was an outdoor living room in a climate that promised not to take over with grunge and kudzu. When we got home we drew a picture of our portal, complete with a porch swing. A place where we could sit and take in the sunset, watch the lingering light and where our children could play out of the harsh afternoon sun of summer. I could imagine hearing the squeak of the swing's chains as I read Mother Goose to them. Looking out over the dark purple masses of the Jemez mountains.

I also fell in love with Dr. Menge's gates, called *zaguan gates*. They were double sized, big enough to run a wagon through. There was no place to put such a thing in our plan; it required a large interior courtyard. Maybe the next house, I said aloud, never for a second believing we'd be building another.

Our final plan was laid in place by the unmovable certainty of the zome as the central room of our home. We had a large kitchen in mind, something with a fireplace at the end. We drew picture after picture until we had something that was a cross between a hacienda fireplace and a Moroccan hut with a low slung living room. It suited us. As we had planned, from the fireplace in the kitchen to the fireplace in the zome, we would pass through three major arches: one Mayan arch and two rounded arches.

One other was Egyptian in style, the third was more or less free form, or as the current expression went "organic."

The closer we got to the sculpting aspect, the rounded door frames and details, the more excited we became.

The walls, constructed of mud bricks, would be twenty-four inches thick stabilized with straw feel. We decided we'd make the adobes ourselves. *Somebody stop us. Please!*

We'd seen the molds for making adobes at our neighbor's house in Corrales. The incubator for our adobe bricks, wooden squares that would hold the wet mud, were like over-sized Coca-Cola crates. When the mud dried in the unforgiving sun, the form could be turned on its side, pulled away. The adobes then turned on their sides dried until thoroughly baked. Just like baking cookies, I thought, without the benefit of egg whites. Everything sounded so Betty Crocker simple until we began this back-breaking process.

When the price of the well came in at a higher cost, more than we'd imagined, we were scrambling to justify the expenses; underneath we quaked with the feel of buyer's regret. But working with Steve had bolstered our confidence: the enthusiasm for our scheme despite the evidence that neither of us had ever built anything.

We had to start with the footings, possibly the most boring part of the project. Steve had warned us that footings for the zome had to be *exact,* the walls plumb, or the panels that were attached to the adobe walls wouldn't fit. As the panels were pre-cut at Zomeworks, we were going to assemble the entire zome onto our adobe walls in one day. The idea of a roof, shade, all happening in one day was a bit of a *milagro* to me.

But first the footings. Digging into hard-packed caliche earth is completely unyielding, the shovel reverberated in my hands. Finally, we decided we needed picks to break into this rugged terrain. Even with picks we made such slow process, I wanted to throw in the shovel and move into a trailer. But the gravelly voice of Eleanor Roosevelt reminded me I had to *do that which I thought I couldn't do.* As I picked and chipped away, I thought of the impossible things I'd already done in my life, like *Alice in Wonderland* who was told to imagine six impossible things before breakfast. I counted birthing children as two of those impossible things. A woman doesn't really think too hard about the size of her pelvis and the watermelon that will eventually pass through it. It's much nicer to think about the eye of the needle and the camel. That thought is somehow less visceral and softer than the truth of childbirth. But here I was in labor again without the benefit of having the fun of getting pregnant.

"Remind me to stand up straight," I said to Lee as I gave the ground another swipe. "Otherwise, at the end of this project I'll look like Quasimodo."

"We *were* warned that the footings were the hardest part of building with adobe," Lee said.

I could feel the vibration zinging through my arms as I hit the earth with the pick. I learned some useful Spanish curse words to amplify my feelings, words: *chinga, puta.*

Each day I allowed myself a quota of ten whines, then I'd go back to the task at hand. It took us weeks to dig the footings for the zome. Along the way we'd get advice from other builders who confirmed that digging the foundations *was* the hardest part.

This thought was gratifying, but my great desire to see walls go up would have to be gratified later. This was a bitch. No other word for it. I hated to say it so early in this stage of building, but I really wanted help. If we could just get this part done, then we could have the zome up and actually have shade. I'd also have the sense that our building was getting somewhere, we weren't just a cosmic joke. My sense of self was at stake here. A failure wasn't even a possibility. I had to keep embracing that old Eleanor Roosevelt notion of gumption. Maybe I chose Eleanor as my role model because my father hated FDR so much. During protracted, painful dinners in our home in New Orleans seated at a table that felt like the size of a football field. I'd often invoke Eleanor when Daddy went into one of his racist rages. She taught me to forbear.

In order to comfort myself, I often stopped to stop and look at where we were in the cosmos. We were in the ante room of the *Sandia Mountains* with a staggering view in front of us. Sometimes I lost sight of the sight. When my vision blurred, the world disappeared like salt in water. I was continually thirsty, but the water from the faucet was always hot. Ice doesn't last long in the desert. Simple rules of the universe were falling into place for me. I tried not to ask myself what I was thirsting for.

Occasionally I'd get a great gift, something out there on the desert floor moved. It was the first road runner I'd ever seen, as comical as the cartoon version depicted it, darting in and out of the junipers, late for an important date. I loved the idea of the road runner as it was my father-in-law's nick name. My Paw Dad, as I called him, was just like that, speedy, efficient. I worked at Ostrich speed, plugged away at projects. Lee was like his dad and got more digging done in half my time. But then, if I kept my pace, I figured Lee's energy would meet me round the bend and I'd be like Tom Sawyer and get somebody else to paint the fence. I was saving my energy for the walls.

Meanwhile, there was plenty to think about there in the frying sun. For example, a warning post outside a public out house: The following creatures inhabit this humble abode. Beware of rattlesnakes, coral snakes, whip snakes, vinegaroons (what was that?), centipedes, ticks, mites, black widows, homed toads, Gila monsters, red ants, fire ants, crickets, giant desert scorpions and tarantulas. Enjoy.

Up close and personal a tarantula is a horror film. I hated to classify a natural being like that. What did he say about me? But once I discovered there weren't poisonous, I could hunker down and study this beast, hairy and brown like a kiwi. He had an odd movement, like a crane lifting its legs or oddly reminding me of a toy machine I used to frequent in New Orleans in Audubon Park. Put in a quarter and watch the crane hover over cheap toys made in Japan. Once the crane had chosen the toy it dropped it into a slot and bingo, I was the happy owner of a fake baby bottle. Just what I wanted. It was the studied movement of the crane that called back when I saw the spider's gait.

Deliberate in its journey, light footed and balanced. I later learned that the Indian culture believes the creatrix of all things is called Spider Woman. Not like the cartoon Spiderman, this sacred mama will either bestow blessings or give you a life like Job. I was learning about the cosmology each day. *Please God, even if you are a spider, don't give me the life of Job. I'll never use an exterminator, bug spray or in any way intrude on webs. Amen.*

I would have thought that having underground utilities, electricity and telephone, wouldn't be such a hassle. Once the trenches from the highway carrying "juice" were dug, the electricity and the phone lines could lie downside by side. Cover the trench, have no ugly wires overhead.

But this didn't happen. The phone company didn't show up, thus making the closing of the trench with only our electricity in place a sad moment. Sadder still when they explained a month later it would cost us about $4,000 to retrench for the phone lines. Our expense. That, I calculated, would make each call from here until my children graduated from high school about $20 per call. Here is where I'd be: out on the mesa with two small children, no telephone. What do I do? Smoke signals? Morse code?

One of the more interesting facts I picked up in a motel drawer during our trek out West was a book about the Mormon faith: a combination of a modern romance and the Koran called, *"Let No Man Write My Epitaph."* These were the virtues as it was explained. It gave the husbands in this celestial marriage, permission to lasso in as many fillies who had the following traits: honesty, truth, chastity, temperance, virtue and, according to some notes scribbled in the margin "be sure you pick a good one, have yourself a shopping spree." There were some crude sketches also in the margin of acceptable positions one could have with each and every one. These crude depictions were things I've never seen before and of course, never in the Bible.

Living on a mesa isn't like being in Lassie's neighborhood, especially when a child goes missing. There's no screen door to stand in front of and call your child's name in one direction and then another. It was all points of the compass. While we were whacking away at the earth, digging the foundations, Morgan was off and running. He had road runnered across the hill. Even running at top speed we couldn't catch up with him. He was part Gingerbread Man, part monkey and it didn't make me happy to see his baby sister watch him like a squid, one big eye gathering information. I knew when she was also up and running, we would have to contend with children who might have to be put on leashes.

On a foray to bring Morgan back we noticed an odd structure several hills over.

We caught him dashing down to the arroyo, stood staring, momentarily, as an odd structure invited closer scrutiny.

"What is that?" I asked directing my finger at something that looked like a cement covered pointed hat, a witch's hat.

"I think that's something called 'the free form,' a commune, more or less," Lee said grabbing Morgan by the straps of his Oshkosh overalls.

"Less than more," I replied staring at the sci-fi set two hills over. It looked as if a passing spaceship had dumped its trash, the mess falling any old way-a galactic junk heap.

"Who lives there?" I asked. "Guess we'll find out," he said. And we did.

One evening after the Sandias had rouged like a night light; we called it quits and decided to introduce ourselves to the people in the puzzling structure called the 'free form.' The earth around this structure was slick and white with gypsum plaster. Wooden poles formed something like a teepee steeple and at the entrance of the place I jumped at the raucous squawking of a rubbery looking chicken. Chicken wire encircled a barnyard with random bowls of feed and water layered in dust. *Caliche,* the top layer of earth in New Mexico, has a talc quality. It is fine and white and blows continually. Because the earth was overblown with *caliche,* I didn't see all the broken stained glass, nails and barbed wire. Buckets filled with some white substance were everywhere.

The entire structure sloped. Not one single straight up and down plumb line. It was like the sets from the noir film the *Cabinet of Dr. Caligari.* Around this junk pile a central shaft of four or five cement columns anchored the sprawling framework. I fully expected bison drawings and petroglyphs on the wall as we entered the place, each of us carrying a child. Even though it was dark in there, just a few hanging light bulbs, I could make out steel and wood beams radiating out from the columns. The truss, spanning one room, was made of car wheel rims welded with pipes. The entire place sloped at odd angles and I had the creepy feeling the inhabitants were anticipating the end of the world. I had a pre-experience of what it would take to live in utter post-war chaos.

In a corner, a woman whose face was half covered with tangled dark hair stared at me, or perhaps beyond me. Something furry scraped my leg. I jumped in time to avoid being pissed on by a Billy goat. Morgan, delighted with this play land, squirmed to get at buckets of sudsy stuff. Just then a man emerged from behind a hanging Mexican blanket wearing a loin cloth. He picked up a bong, sucked and left. The last rays of the sun turned the walls of the hovel bright green, yellow and red. Three quarters of the room was stained glass. Another man stepped out from behind the plastered partitions. "Dude," he said, "I'm Jerry."

We introduced ourselves as the new neighbors. With the dim light I could barely make him out. In this twilight he resembled a shadow puppet against the white plastered wall. His Bozo hair thickened into a bristly aura about his head and glowed reddish.

"Welcome to Sweetwater," he said licking the end of a joint. "It's called that because it costs like a mother fucker to drill." He offered us a hit of his dope.

"Yeah," Lee said. "We found that out.

I already felt I was on a bongo board with the lilting walls and the at sea feel of the place. I didn't need any more unbalance.

We told him we'd just gotten our final papers on the land and were starting the foundations and making our own adobes. In the twilight, the small orange circle of Jerry's joint glowed, illuminating his face as he puffed.

"So," Lee began, "where'd you get the idea for your place?"

"Two thousand and One. You know, the movie?" He spoke and vacuumed dope. "Like when the dude splits out of the satellite heading for Jupiter-all those different types of infra-red colors, like a plane zooming through the Grand Canyon at full tilt.

What's created with a house is more or less synonymous to the cell structure of the body. You dig?

"You mean the stained glass is like the infra-red?" Light from the stained glass bounced all over the wonky walls.

"Kinda," he said exhaling. "But see the stained glass," he arched his arm. "It's like jewelry. That's what we make here. It was natural to live in what you make."

"What holds this place together?" Lee asked simultaneously grabbing Morgan's shirt to keep him from stepping on a shard of blue spiked glass. Lee pointed to the vast amount of open sky throughout the structure. "And what do you do about rain?"

"It's organic, man." He rolled another joint. "See the wood is covered with tar paper and chicken wire and the whole mother is plastered with gypsum mixed with perlite."

Lee asked again. "And the rain?"

THIRST

"Most it rains here is about ten inches a year. I mean, it isn't critical."

Sunset was dancing through the cockeyed structure as we spoke, giving me the feeling of spun-out nights in the Fillmore Auditorium in San Francisco.

"How big is this place?" I asked.

"About 5,000 square feet," answered a female voice from behind the plastered partition.

"My old lady," Jerry explained nodding in her direction.

"She's doing school shit. Teaches in Algodones."

I couldn't see her, so I quickly imagined her as a hippie version of Our Miss Brooks hooked up to a hookah pipe.

Lilah woke up and started to cry. "What's her name?" Jerry said.

"Lilah."

"Far out. Cool name. There's a commune named that up by Truchas."

"We know," I replied. "We stayed there during a blizzard last spring."

"Far out."

We'd just scored some points for camping out in a wild commune so far off the grid when we got stranded there I didn't know if we were still in New Mexico. I didn't tell him we left as soon as the snow melted.

Before we left Jerry showed us two or three walls that didn't connect, so the entire wing was abandoned.

"Kids want to see Jon-Jon the Jewish chicken?" Jerry asked. "Next time," I said. A Jewish chicken?

When we fell into bed in our rented home in Corrales, before falling asleep I said, "Why do I think there's no book club out here?"

We finally met Jerry's "old lady," the woman behind the ferro cement curtain in the "free form." She was puttering down the road in their red VW bug off to teach in a nearby school. Her dashboard was lined with joints and she was sucking the life out of one when she stopped. Her lips puckered to hold it in place. "Lost my roach clip," she said by way of introduction. Tossed the tiny remains out the window and idled her thunking car.

"We're making adobes, digging trenches for the foundations."

"Heavy," she replied.

Dallas had a sweet smile and a way of rolling her eyes upwards I found engaging, a nonverbal "wow" kind of expression. Her dark tousled hair fell to shoulder length.

"Want a hit?" She began smoking one of the pre-rolled joints. "I'm nursing, thanks."

"Kids can get behind dope," she assured me. "Not *my* kids."

"Well, gotta go. If you ever want to mellow those kids down, call."

Jerry showed up on our work site one afternoon and gave a small wave of the hand. He was wearing a carpenter's apron, divided by wide pockets. In the canvas partitions I noticed a mixture of dope, nails and vials of pills. He walked over to our building plans, shook the paper then asked, "What's this?"

"Our building plans." "Looks like square walls."

"That's right," Lee replied. He stopped and showed him the large rectangular plans for the kitchen that led towards the zome, the heart of our home.

"Fuck man, that looks like a *hacienda*. Like something a square dude from Illinois would build-the guy with the brick house and Quaid fence... we call him Mr. Military Industrial complex. Guy's a pain in the ass."

I turned to see his Gabby Hays mouth, his lips, tomato ripe on the verge of splitting.

"So you won't need this." He threw down some curious cylinders.

"What's that?" Lee asked.

"Dynamite, it's a welcome to the neighborhood gift."

"For?"

"Man, just stick the dynamite in the hillside of the *arroyo* and wherever it blows, you build around it. Simpler than that adobe shit, cheaper too." He rolled another joint. "Like what we did with the 'free form.' He pointed to their intergalactic space junk a few hills over.

"We'd rather do something more traditional, except for the zome."

"I see that," he said turning in disgust. "So, you guys are constructing a Taco Bell?"

"We like organic," Lee said. "Adobe."

"Dig it. We had about 8,000 adobes, but they all washed away in a rainstorm.

Using scrap is cheaper, easier. You can just leave a wall and come back to it, then go in a totally different direction. Flexible. You dig?"

When my mother referred to "foundations," she meant girdles and bras. Foundations, or footings, in an adobe are crucial. A certain foot of adobe has to be supported underneath by a masonry structure or the heavy adobes will mash down. It's that simple. Think of a cake falling after you take it out of the oven.

The cement blocks have to be deep enough, below the frost line, or moisture will get in and freeze with the possibility of lifting the entire house, then you will end up with cracked walls as the house settles.

To reinforce the cement poured into the footings, rebar has to be hammered in. If we'd used only one adobe, normally about 10" thick, the footings had to be 3" wider on each side of the wall. Severe winter weather has to be reckoned into this first step, we learned, or your walls will freeze and crack. Since we were using two adobes, our woe was doubled. If the land you are building on isn't level, then you have to build forms and pour in concrete. Most sane people used machinery to dig the trenches. The first step for us was hand-to-hand combat.

In a week we'd made such a pitiful dent in our foundations I wanted to cry. I felt as if I'd been using a jackhammer all day, my body hummed like a tuning fork. Several people had driven by and given their opinions and thoughts. "Footings are the toughest part, amigo," one fellow builder told us. Another cheerfully said we might build our house ourselves, but we'd never stay married. This piece of advice came so regularly I was thinking of putting it on a needlepoint pillow. The stress of this phase was making us both cranky. If this was the beginning of our building odyssey, what could possibly lay ahead? And with each slam of the pick or shovel I started having serious doubts about the entire project but the worst was related to the fact that our house would be made of mud. It was a Three Little Pigs thought as I recalled the dumb pigs that made their houses of straw and other flimsy materials. Only the smart pig went for the brick, but it wasn't an adobe brick, and he had a modest, smart-pig sized house.

I was thinking about the wolf coming down the chimney of smart pig's house on a Friday afternoon. My mind was a carousel of doubt.

What if my parents were right and we ran out of money. I'm glad my mother couldn't see the way money was flying. Both of my parents had lived through Depression and had embossed the picture of folks cold and hungry standing in bread lines. We were idiots, our heads in some crazy dream world that would crash around us one day.

I looked at the mess scattered among the junipers: broken rebar, buckets of slush, trowels and shovels thrown into what would be the center of our sacred zome. I closed my eyes against our vanishing dream.

I had other scary thoughts, too. Our babysitter, Delores, was flakey and often when we came home, I'd see yet another color on her toe nails. I had a good idea how she spent her time. On a few occasions I sniffed the scent of something like Bryl Cream on my pillow and wondered if she were using our bed to entertain her boyfriends while our children darted in and out of the whizzing traffic on Corrales Road.

My father had a rule, many rules. One crucial regulation which came from who knows where was "You can't quit something once you start it. No ifs, ands or buts about it."

"What's wrong?" Lee put his shovel down.

"Oh, not much. I'm just having a nervous breakdown."

"Want to tell me about it?"

"I hardly see the kids. When we come home, I'm so tired it's all I can do to put a meal together then that worthless Delores hasn't done a single thing like fold the laundry. She didn't *wash* the diapers, all I asked her to do was fold them. And there's breakfast dishes still stacked up. My pillow smells like a Chinese whore house."

"Wait. What?" Lee put his hand on my shoulder. "Ease up."

"What if we get so obsessed with this project we lose all contact with our children? What if we come home and find Lilah wearing a training bra?

"Okay, I see you need a break, your mind is going way into the stratosphere."

I started to cry. "Sometimes I think about being a child again in Audubon Park playing with sisters and brother, feeding the swans and riding the swan boat, or on the carousel. If we don't do normal things with our kids they may turn out to be dirt eaters or suck exhaust pipes like that kid in the village." I threw down my shovel. "Just a normal weekend at home. Is that asking so much?"

"You make me sound like I'm forcing you to do this."

"That's not what I mean and you know it." I threw a rusty trowel at the mud pit. "Somebody asked me what we were doing other than the house and I nearly screamed at them *There is no other. Nothing.*"

"Okay, let's sit down a minute. Here's the facts." He turned me around so we had eye contact. I didn't want him to see my trembling lip. "If we don't keep at this, it just won't get done. If the walls and bond beam don't go up before the cold weather, we have a hovel on our hands. If we bring the kids out here we will get nothing done. We'll be chasing after Morgan and at the end of the day trying to find the tools he's lost. Money. Lost time. And who's to say this place is safer than home?"

"Thanks, I needed that." I didn't want to give voice to my fears-- the kids and what they might get into in a flash.

"Okay, a weekend off. No building. We can do that."

I looked at him, searching his face to see if he was disgusted with this decision or if he got it, how unraveled I'd become. He lifted a hair from across my face. He saw my distress. "Don't lose hope," he said.

"You mean that elusive thing with wings?" But I knew he was listening.

On the way home I asked, "What if we cast the coins from the I Ching, just to see where we are on this impossible journey?"

"Okay by me." We slowed down to make way for Jerry's VW bug. "Quitting?" Jerry asked, squinting into the sun.

"We need a break; those footings are wiping us out." Lee tilted his head towards our site.

"Footings are a bitch," said Jerry. "Dig it?"

I looked at Jerry's face and thought about how odd it was, sometimes looking like a disintegrating Halloween pumpkin, and others looking benign. Once he turned toward me and I thought about how, in a bonnet, he could pass himself off like a little old lady, like Toad disguising himself as a washer woman in *Wind in the Willows*. Jerry, I decided, was a shape shifter.

We parted company, not returning until Monday morning.

That night as Morgan dismantled the abandoned chicken coop in our rented home in Corrales, we took out three coins and tossed them, then read the hexagram from the *Book of Changes*. "Perseverance Furthers," we read again. Not terribly comforting.

Nothing seemed to be changing. That night Lee left a note on my pillow a quote from Faulkner, from a book he'd be teaching in the fall. "I mind I used to think that hope was about all folks had, only now I'm beginning to believe that that's about all anybody needs--jest hope."

We were driving along the highway when I turned to him. "Let's name our new home "Jest Hope." He smiled. We were back on track. As we drove up to our land that Monday morning only slightly rested from our AWOL weekend, a sidewinder rattler wiggled in front of our car making something like the letter "J" in the dirt. I couldn't believe how he blended in with the earth. And he seemed to be sliding towards our building site. I'd seen two snakes getting it on earlier that year. They were entwined in a juniper looking like a caduceus. Perhaps this was one of their offspring. I tried not to think about all the predators we knew about in our living habitat. Once I'd found possibly the ugliest bug I'd ever seen. It almost looked like a baby in shape, grotesque in its fetus-like form. Jerry happened to be there that day. He picked it up and looked at it. "A vinegaroon. Groovy," he said blowing it off into the universe with a blessing of home grown.

`As we got closer to the house after a restful weekend, ready to forge ahead with our trenching and finally foundations, it looked as if a dragon had been dragging its tail all over our land, snapping it alligator style and having a good old Louisiana stomp. First, we noticed frenzied tracks all over the dusty earth, crisscrossed tire impressions like tennis shoe skid marks on a basketball court. Or perhaps the Hell's Angels had a convention over the weekend, running their bikes all over the land.

My first hope was the phone company had a turn of heart and was coming to put the trenches in for phone access. But at first glance, I couldn't see any trenches leading up to the site. So we walked around the beginnings of the footings until we got to the section where our children's rooms would be. Then there was a dramatic change in elevation. I was stunned. Somebody had dug out what looked like a swimming pool in the space slated for Morgan and Lilah's bedroom. The excavation was so deep, if l stood where their bed would be, I'd have to climb a ladder to see out the window. Lee said it succinctly: "What the fuck!"

We had to jump down into the hole where we clearly saw the metal footprints of some large piece of machinery.

"Somebody's mistaken our property for a community swimming-pool," I said. "How could that happen at night?" Lee said looking at the hard evidence of the teeth marks of the mechanical beast.

"Is this some kind of warning?" I wondered out loud. "Like what?"

"I don't know. Any chance this land was cursed by the Indians? Maybe we've hit their sacred burial ground or something."

We sat together, mystified, letting our legs dangle over the pit. Piles of dirt formed pyramids around us.

After a while I came up with an idea: "Let's sell this dirt to the people who make runaway truck ramps."

We didn't even know how to proceed. Now the only way to put foundations in would be to pour massive amounts of cement into a form. And the room would be at the end of a ramp. I was thinking of the word cockeyed, recalling the fun house at our New Orleans Amusement Park, Pontchartrain Beach. It wasn't long before our questions were answered.

We lapsed into great silences inert with the mess in front of us. "Who would do this to us? You think that guy who owns the brick house, the Quaid fence near the highway would try to scare us off?" We'd heard from Jerry the guy raised cane about everything. His "handle" in our neighborhood, according to Jerry, was "Mr. Military Industrial Complex."

I stopped talking and tried to read Lee's face. "I swear, it's a Nixon thing. He's got long haired hippies on the run. Just the other day I passed a bread van with writing on the side that said, "In God we trusted, in Texas we got busted."

"Don't fall into paranoia, please," he said.

There were so few houses out our way, it would be difficult to know why our building would threaten anyone. There was a trailer right off the highway where an Indian woman and a Scottish man lived with a bunch of kids. Close to them was a round adobe house and then another trailer that had pathetic barbed wire they did have rather large teeth. We were talking about the donkey when we heard footsteps.

A swaggering Jerry smoking a spliff the size of a cigar, showed up at the sight. In the bright sun I could see the roadmap of his face, weathered as a baseball mitt. His crystalline eyes bounced around his head.

"So, what'd you think, man?"

"Mind telling me what happened here?" Lee asked pointing to the cavern.

"Some dude left his keys in a backhoe, so we dropped a little speed, some acid," he smiled, "we work great behind speed. You can work all night on that shit."

"I see." Lee was pulsing with anger. "So you feel okay about turning our kid's bedroom into an Olympic sized swimming pool?"

"Fuck, man. Can't you even fucking say thank you?"

We peered over the pit together, sat down in silence. Jerry shrugged, turned his back and walked around muttering about in gratitude.

"Oh, thanks. Thanks for our own personal Grand Canyon. *Chinga*, fuck, shit, mother fucker, piss, crap and *merde*. I feel better now," Lee said.

Jerry swaggered around the pit, pride in his assessment of the work they'd done in the dark.

"Like just use that dynamite, man. You could blow another hole next to this one, ferro cement the thing. You'd have a house in a week."

"How about we don't *want* to do that?" Lee said. "Don't you ask somebody before you go around rearranging their house plans?"

"Man, like you got to go with the flow."

"Oh, please," I said. "See this is *no* flow. This is a stopped sewage pipe. Do you get we like the idea of up and down walls?"

I held my arm up, so he'd get an idea of a straight wall.

what a straight wall might look like. "We don't want to feel dizzy, seasick just getting to our bedrooms."

"Hey, like I just saved you some bucks. You'll never have a problem with a stopped toilet. Look, man. Gravity will pull all your shit clear to your septic tank." "Isn't this a little extreme to avoid stopped plumbing?"

Lee asked.

"And what about all these hills of dirt? They look like Indian burial mounds."

Jerry pitched what was left of his spliff onto the desert floor. "You know, out here when someone does you a favor, we say, like thanks, man."

I could see this request wasn't going down well with Lee. I intervened.

"Okay. Truce. Don't do us any more favors, please. If you get a hold of a piece of machinery, go dig out someone else's house site. What do you think would have happened if you'd done this to somebody else? They would be thanking you? Come on."

Jerry's anger wafted off him like cheap perfume. He turned his back and started walking to his free form. "Go ahead, man. Fuck up the neighborhood with your Taco Bell house. How about a car wash?"

I felt sure by the time he reached home he had some other choice comparisons. But we, in the meantime, had to cope with mess he and Merry Pranksters had created.

FOOTINGS

We started talking to friends at the Thunderbird Bar about our little "overtrench" problem. Everyone said the same thing. We'd have to get a cement truck to pour the foundations. We weighed it all against two factors 1. money and 2. time.

The echoing voice of Dr. Menge, house builder extraordinaire, reminded us we had to get our walls up before the first freeze. And so far we hadn't started making our adobes. So we hired a truck, built the forms reinforced by rebar which encircled our future house like a big rusty bracelet. While the truck poured the cement into the trenches, we frantically troweled so the foundations were even. Although it was fine in our neighborhood to build wonky looking houses, we were still going for the gold: plumb.

The cement dried for a week. We had fun writing things in the drying cement, as if we thought they might be discovered in the next millennium, our house cracked open like a pharoh' s tomb with the secrets of crazy Americans embedded in the earth like the caves in Altamira or the scratchings on the walls at Chaco Canyon.

We hate Nixon. Peace. Vote Democrat. The Grateful Dead slept here. Elvis is alive and lives in Tucumcari. Jimmy Hoffa is buried here. Dick Clark is homosexual. Words of this nature might make a person in the future pause and reflect on our era. Maybe. At any rate, we had made it past the huge hurdles, despite the help of Jerry. We were ready to make our adobes.

We finished the foundations for the zome first because we figured having that structure up in one day would give our spirits a boost. Shade. What a word, so deep and rich.

Mud for adobes has to be sifted before it is mixed with water. Ideally, we would have used a cement mixer, but we were short on funds after we paid the well drilling folks, and so we made a mud pit and had dump trucks of dirt unloaded on our site.

We'd found a guy named Zeke who delivered the dirt from the Rio Grande Valley, the *bosque.* Zeke was an elderly Spanish gent with a white moustache and a deep laugh reminding me of someone on the set of *The Treasure of the Sierra Madre.*

Everyone seemed to know this guy, but at that time we hadn't configured the interconnection of the building world yet, how everybody had a line on something whether it was dirt or beams or rebar. Zeke had a line on everything. He was the Hispanic equivalent of the father from "Sanford and Son" double and triple dealing adobes, *vigas,* (beams for the ceiling) and used rebar, "much cheaper," he told us. Zeke let us know just what he was thinking by raising his thick eyebrow that seemed to span his entire face. His favorite expression, "Oh, really?"

The dirt Zeke ferried had a rich riverbed consistency, perfect for mud pies or adobes. He dumped the load near the well. I was becoming a *connoisseur* of mud, running the earth through my fingers admiring the deep dark color, "mud *nouveau,"* I said to Lee approving of the latest batch without any detectable shards of glass. Because I was mixing dirt and water with my feet in a big pit, it was crucial to me to know just what was in that load.

First we sifted, then re-sifted. Then I hosed water into the center of the mound, the way French cooks begin a batch of bread. Next, I climbed on top of the heap and began my back and forth hoeing operation until I began to disappear in the mud trough. After the mud was adobe ready, we poured it, bucketful by bucketful into the molds to dry.

One afternoon I noticed billows of dust coming down our spit of land. For a few minutes he watched us, his head hanging out of the window. Then Zeke dismounted his beat-up blue truck.

"You better off buying adobes from me, Johnson." He nudged one of our not quite-dry bricks. "Mine are thicker, stronger."

"We're doing fine," Lee said.

"See when the rains come, if you don't get those adobes off the ground you're going to have a big mud hole on your hands."

I wheeled another load of heavy mud to our pit as Lee dumped a sliding mud fall into the forms. With a trowel I smoothed the layer of mud into the form and suddenly I knew Lee was listening to Zeke, but it took a minute for him to respond.

"Maybe we'll get bricks from you later, Zeke."

"Later might be too late, my friend." Zeke wagged his toothpick back and forth, thumped the door of his truck then left.

The mud had to be the perfect consistency. Too slurpy and it wouldn't dry properly, we'd have to start over. Too many failures and we wouldn't have enough adobes to build our house. We were running against time. And, because we were tense and tired, we got a little sloppy with our sifting and resifting, sometimes just unloading the wheelbarrow, adding water and me jumping into the mud hole to begin my sacred mud dance. It had already snowed in Santa Fe, a quirk of Nature, but a reminder of our timetable deadline with Jack Frost.

By the end of September, the nights get cold in the mountains and the mud begins to freeze. A frozen adobe brick chips, fissures, cracks and crumbles. These were going to be our walls.

I look back on photos of us in the mud pit, our backs burned from the sun. My hair is bleached white. The picture evokes the sound of the hoe slurping back and forth in the mud pit. Back and forth incessant rhythm until all the lumps disappear. At first, I felt the rocking sensation of repetitive motion almost lulling. And then, after weeks of back aches I felt like a member of a chain gang. But we were actually making our own adobes. There was a huge sense of pride in that. Not only were we going to build our own house, we were making the bricks as well. Eleanor Roosevelt would have doffed her hat to me.

It took about two weeks for the mud to dry enough to lift the heavy form, then we lifted it, a task in itself and the first stage of adobe making was complete. Next the adobes had to be dry enough to turn on their sides like three-month-old babies. They cured there another week or so, then they were ready to be a wall. Our wall. Our house. Our baby. There are many hazards in mixing mud in a pit with your feet. First, I might be mistaken for Lucille Ball as she stomped grapes in a peasant's outfit. There was also the danger of messing up my back from bending, but finally the things I thought wouldn't be a problem were. I was stomping around in my pig pen one day when a sharp pain shot through my foot. I hosed off the mud to discover a deep gash. We had to dig through the mud to find the offender, and sure enough, it was a large shard of glass. I worried about all the things my mother used to foretell: lockjaw was high on the list. My mother was a typical fifties mother who always believed the worst would happen. If we weren't careful with pencils, for example, we might not just fall down and break the pencil, we'd poke out our eyes, My sister was scratched by a cat we didn't recognize in our neighborhood and for three days my mother was convinced she'd contracted rabies. All of these echoes sent me to the medical facility in Bernalillo where I got a tetanus shot then bought a cheap pair of tennis shoes to protect my feet. About a week later I was scratched by a piece of barbed wire that looked as if it might have been a remnant from World War II. Our carelessness, lack of deep sifting maneuvers, now came back to bite me again. As I sat in the waiting room to get my leg looked at, a guy across the way, having discovered the source of my pain, regaled me with facts about barbed wire. "Gal, I'm telling you there's two thousand types of barbed wire. Hell," he said, "there's even a barbed wire museum in Texas."

"I'll be sure and stop off there on my next trip home," I said.

Then a woman dressed in long skirt, a rebozo-type blouse and long pig tails got into it with the barbed wire connoisseur.

"Barbed wire ruined the West."

"What?" he said nearly coming off his chair.

"Kept everything penned in. Cattle can't graze naturally. Like being in jail."

"Remember the Alamo," he countered back, apropos of nothing.

And so I sat waiting for my leg appraisal over the gun fire of ideologies, no longer connected to reason. The final word from the gent was "Don't tread on me, you dirty hippie.

There's a reason they call you the wasted generation. You're wasted on drugs, you waste your life, your time."

"How about you, Agnew lover? She said, waving a Life Magazine at hin. "I suppose you think the Nixon and Agnew are pure as the driven snow?"

During the crossfire I imagined the bumper stickers on the back of the young woman's car. Maybe "Give Peace a Chance." Our decade had wafted into Crosby, Stills and Nash abandoning the raucous music of the sixties like Cream or The Doors. I remembered a poignant quote from a member of the Hog Farm Commune, Wavy Gravy. "War is an odd way to get acquainted." I liked that.

I was glad to get back to the tranquility of be good to leave the planet in peace.

The kids were definitely growing up in our absence. Lilah watched her brother and did anything he told her to. "Taste this, Lilah," he told her once offering her a spoon of mushy mud before I could jerk it out of his hand.

I tried to keep our Creole heritage alive by giving them useful table manner proverbs like "Spoon goes to bowl's house. Bowl doesn't go to spoon's house." This one, I discovered stuck when Lilah at aged three corrected Morgan. "Spoon goes to bowl's house, Morgan." She learned fast.

I thought perhaps when the zome went up we could bring them out to the site where they could play in the shade. I was still afraid of sun over-exposure, particularly for Lilah. She was the kind of kid who immediately ripped off any hat put on her head. I often forgot that their great-great-grandmother was tough, part Cherokee. She already had the female trait from Lee's family of cocking one hip and placing her arm at an angle. I have many photos of Lee's grandmother and great grandmother in this bossy stance. Nothing made Lilah angrier than being told by her brother that she was a "bitsy bosser."

My husband's family owned a plantation in Mississippi near Meridian called Millbrook. Although I never met my husband's great grandmother there were stories aplenty about her. From time to time the folks, the "help," would dash out of the house swearing they heard Mrs. Kramer tapping her cane as she marched down the hallway. Mrs. Kramer ran the plantation single-handed sending timber down the Chickasawhay River to Mobile. Lilah had a look about her eyes that reminded me of old photographs of this resilient woman who walloped mule teams. In family lore it was said the only person who worked harder than Mrs. Kramer was the boll weevil.

I thought about the complications of having the kids on the building sight. We'd have to keep snacks that didn't go off, peanut butter, I thought would be a good choice, and of course, plenty of cold water. At our rented house in Corrales they had shade and could dabble around in their wading pool. In two months, they'd gone through two wading pools as Morgan brought his sturdy yellow Tonka trucks in the water with him and ran them full tilt around the sides like a race track.

I always took both of them to the food co-op so they could see all the barrels of grains, the bins of spaghetti and swirly pasta and their favorite, the machine that turned peanuts into peanut butter. For some reason that transformation thrilled them as the peanut butter swirled down into a jar like ice cream. One day Morgan watched this procedure closely. He turned to me and said with his engaging smile, "Doo doo."

When we left California the phrase of the week was "don't lay your trip on me." Now there was a new more refined consciousness sweeping the land. I was made aware of not wasting water not only by the people in the village, but also by the folks at the food co-op. No use telling them water was the biggest commodity in Louisiana, right next to mosquitoes.

Suddenly, since an event called "Earth Day" it seemed the whole world had turned into one big health food co-op. I now made my own yogurt and grew my own sprouts. My father said food like that was all hippie "gabboldygook. All sprouts did was stop up your toilet." Jerry would likely have agreed if they'd ever gotten into a conversation. I never saw Jerry eat anything bordering on healthy and I had to remind him not to give the kids soda or candy. "Hey, man, you only live once," he told me.

Meanwhile back at the rust ranch, the weather beat down on us. At lunch we were forced to crawl under juniper bushes for shade. Our car was so hot even with towels on the steering wheel we couldn't touch it until the sun set. "Remember the tin Quonset huts they used for prisoners in "The Bridge Over the River Kwai?" I said biting into a stale sandwich. "And just think, come winter it will be as brutally cold as it is hot."

"But we'll have twenty-four inches of insulation between us and the snow," Lee the eternal optimist, said.

"Maybe we should consider buying already made adobes," I said enjoying a small breeze.

"Costs too much," Lee said.

At the end of the day we hosed down our wheelbarrow and the wooden frame.

As we lifted the heavy frame Lee said, "Zeke said to keep this thing clean."

Daily the sun beat down on us like a maul. The "Land of Enchantment" was getting less and less enchanting. I couldn't even remember the last time I'd used the word *easy*. Fine caliche dust powdered my arms, blended with my sweat, caked me from head to ankles. Feet already clodded with mud from the pit. Little splotches of dirt dotted my face like beauty marks. Bigger clumps dried in my hair.

"I look awful," I said. "I'd be mistaken as a reject from a German health farm." This was a reference to a place we'd visited in Germany where a hefty hausfraus climbed out of a mud bath looking like the creature from The Black Lagoon.

Lee took my arm, spit on his finger then rubbed a small portal on my arm. He kissed the opening. "Eve," he reminded me, "was made of spit and clay."

At our lunch break under the juniper I suggested we borrow or rent a cement mixer.

"I thought your motto was neither a borrower nor a lender be."

"I wish your memory wasn't so finely turned," I said, flicking a clod of mud off his cheek. "You really missed your calling," I reflected. "With your abacus mind you would have been a great lawyer. I'll bet you could argue for the South in the Civil War, then turn around and make a great case for the North. You could indict a hamburger if you wanted."

"I like verbal battles," he said.

"I know. But sometimes your acuity wears me out. One of the best things about living in a hippy population is they are practically pre-verbal. But I do miss words strung together in engaging ways... just not arguments."

Then I added. "I know you hate for me to remind you but..." I touched a red spot on his forehead. "As my father used to tell you, your skin is too fair to be unprotected. You need to put on some sunscreen."

"Now you're agreeing with your father?"

Sometimes our best communication was through telepathy. Once when Lee was off to the grocery, I remembered an item I forgot to put on the list: coffee. Only one store in Albuquerque sold coffee from Louisiana and we were both addicted to it. I was shoveling mud when I stopped and sent him one thought: *Luzianne, coffee and chicory, the red can.* When he got home I asked, "Did you get it?"

"The coffee? "Yep, that was it."

A little later as we watched the sunset I asked, "Does it ever scare you I can read your mind?"

"Sometimes."

I didn't ask when those "sometimes" moments happened.

It was restful under the juniper. The berries carried a scent almost like a Christmas tree. I liked squeezing the berries and rubbing the blue juice on my arms giving me a tribal look. "Maybe someone will make a movie about aborigines and we can be extras, after all we're already caked with mud." No response.

"How about bartering? Everyone out here barters."

"Care to name our current assets?"

"Two lovely children. A five-year-old Vega station wagon. Two mattresses. A hand-made quilt."

"You forgot the radio."

"Good thing you got your PhD from Stanford," I said curling into fetal position.

We stayed in spoon mode under the tree, the green branches patting us on the back like Eleanor Roosevelt encouraging us to keep fighting on.

Clouds in New Mexico are shape shifters, demons. Gigantic galleons float over the intense sky then drift over the mountains.

Cumulus heaps, cirrus curls, stratus layers, nimbus means rain. But when I think back at the hours I cloud watched as I mixed mud in my pit, one image drifts continually back. It is a drifting curtain that hovers over the land, it is the temptress, the rain the Indians call Walking Rain. It is also known as *Virga*. Rain that never touches ground.

I became intimate with this phenomenon, thinking I might be the one to break the spell, to get this vision to actually fall. The veils of water looked like a transparent gauze covering as it came closer. I could imagine folks seeing the Madonna wrapped in moisture watching over the land. I could also imagine folks like me shaking my fist at the sky, wishing just a spit of moisture would fall, cool me off. It was the old Madonna/whore syndrome, I thought of mouthing the name *puta* towards the advancing mirage. *Puta,* whore. *Virga,* virgin. I got so fixated on *virga,* I began to make up mythologies around her. One went like this: one day Hera was bored, filing her nails. Zeus had pissed her off, another woman. What's new? And so out of spite, revenge and just malice, she told him of their coming child, a girl. He looked at her briefly, somewhat askance as the last child had sprung from his forehead and had given him dreadful headaches.

"This one will be different, she will be forever virgin." When he raised his eyebrow, Hera knew she was on to something. And so one day darling *Virga* appeared, floating over their bed, sweet as rain. He opened his arms wide to welcome his daughter, but she never reached his embrace. No matter how he stretched and screamed she remained at a distance. His anger grew so fierce he hurtled lightning bolts in the nursery.

This had no effect on the untouchable child. And so Hera watched in amusement at the one thing she'd produced that was as relentless as the gadfly.

If we hadn't taken off for lunch that day things might have turned out differently. Inside Anita's restaurant, eating a big honey drenched *sopapilla,* I left all thoughts of the mud pit, the drying adobes, what lay ahead. Families all around us were enjoying every form of chile, sucking down Dos Equis beer and taking a long lunch, which sounded very sane to me.

"I'm beginning to feel like one of those faces on Mount Rushmore," Lee said looking at my dirt cogged arm.

"I always said you were statuesque." He replied.

"We should eat out more often," I said sipping my water.

Lee made a little sign with his thumb and middle finger. "Money."

While we were under the shelter of the restaurant, nature was busy, busy, busy. And we were groggy coming out of the blessed conditioned air into the blaring sun. But something had changed. Clouds banked over the mountains. As we drove closer to the site, a low-flying cloud skimmed over us looking like a manta ray. It wasn't like the clouds in Louisiana that portend "weather." It was as innocent as a lamb. Nothing to worry about, I thought.

I looked into our nursery of baby adobes drying, maturing before my very eyes. Most were lying flat, but some had been dry enough to turn on their sides. They took on a purplish cast at sunset. I stopped counting the amount we'd need, and focused on the number we'd already poured, dried and turned. We'd soon have an impressive stack.

Pride comes before a fall.

Then the cloud, innocent as a baby's bum, bouncy almost white, cast a shadow. I could see the knuckles of the Sandias, how they dug into the land, where the scrub forest had greened and where the rock face glinted. Suddenly, the sky cracked open. It felt as if a thousand tons of water splattered buckets of it feeling like the weight of a hundred elephants. Unmerciful rain. Incessant. Indefatigable, spirit-crushing rain. Rain to beat the band. Cruel rain. Ceaseless, battering, unstoppable boom or bust rain. Gully washer rains that filled the dry riverbeds in the arroyo causing flash floods. We were ambushed, pulling tarps, plastic coverings even raincoats over our drying adobes. I tried to hold the plastic down, support one end with a concrete block, but the winds had picked up and it felt like a hurricane billowing our sails. At one point I even thought of throwing myself over the adobes to save them like some early black and white Russian film, desperate mothers leaping from ice floe to ice floe to save their child. But it wasn't a passing shower, this was the kind of stuff that literally swept children away.

"This is biblical," I yelled over the lashing water. We were no longer on a mesa in the desert; we were at sea battling a squall. Our attempts at protecting our treasure against Mother Nature were hopeless, pitiful. I cried as I watched the adobes disintegrate back into fluid mud. Within an hour our adobe field became an adobe graveyard. Our house was a ruin-in-progress. Our adobe field looked like the abandoned homes of the mysterious Anasazi Indians. And in two hours the sun was shining, baking. I could almost hear distant trickster laughter as the clouds rolled up towards the *Sandias,* rolling home like Old Man River.

A few hours later Zeke appeared, elbow out the truck window, his roving toothpick circumnavigating his mouth. He leaned out, surveyed our disastrous mud flats, our washed-out adobe field.

"See you got some rain," he said.

PART II

As the sun sank across the mesas, our hearts plummeted. We realized we'd have to buy adobes from Zeke. A few days later, he whistled through his toothpick loading them up next to our site, then watched at our pitiful attempts to dig the footings, the foundation for our dream *hacienda*.

As he climbed into his truck he said, "If I was you, Johnson, I'd get me a mixer and hire some help. I got a line on two guys."

"We'll manage," Lee said.

When he'd gone, I asked, "Why does he address you as Johnson, as if I weren't doing anything?"

"It's the culture," he said, slamming a pick into the earth.

The adobes were delivered in silence, neatly stacked and waiting. At this point I didn't have the heart to go back into my mud pit. To catch up we were going to have to buy a cement mixer. We still had to fill in the concrete blocks that sat atop the foundations with cement. Mixing all of that by hand in the wheelbarrow would put our project so far behind we may as well abandon the project and begin again in the Spring. And then there was the mortar to be mixed. Waiting until Spring. That would have been the sensible thing to do.

When I saw an ad in the paper for a cement mixer at half price, I thought our luck was turning around. It was at Sears, how reliable can you get? We hauled it out of the back of our Scout thinking how our trials were coming to an end... something like a sign from God, or in the case of the Southwest, Zeus. As we unpacked it we soon realized why it was half price. The entire engine had to be assembled. The directions were written in such tiny print even with a magnifying glass they were hard to read. But here's the best part: two pages were missing. *Perseverance furthers.* Lee crumpled against the side of the car. "Here's the rule: both of us can't fall apart at the same time. You have a breakdown now," I said, "mine will follow after that. In the meantime, let's get onto this."

I felt as if I'd hit the math section of the SAT exam as I looked at the puzzling directions. Suddenly I felt a presence behind me, silent as a snake. Then a pointed toe edged a bolt towards me onto the flapping thin paper, onto the paragraph I was puzzling through. Jerry leaned down and put a few pieces of the machine together, screwing one thing into another. He never said anything. Pretty soon we were more than halfway done as his mute instructions led us along. It took the entire afternoon, spent in what I'd call Buddhist silence. At the end he handed Lee a joint. The peace pipe was passed.

During the fifties we'd both seen movies about the undead, with titles like *I Walked with a Zombie.* Since we'd both grown up in New Orleans, Voo Doo wasn't a new idea for either of us. And daily I felt more and more possessed. Each day we got to work early, trying to beat the sun's relentless path, following a pattern of mixing mud, troweling it onto a layer of adobe. Carry, tote, hose, carry. The cement mixer wasn't the magical cure I'd been seeking. We were hurrying to get the zome walls up, the promise of roof and shade, the sound of the mixer now slopping mud like some drunk's big tongue slurping around his mouth.

The desert, too, is as relentless as the sea and I'd stop and stare, starved for a break in the monotony. I have a tendency, despite my father's rule, to quit a project before completing it, like my trunk of unfinished sewing projects, wraparound skirts that were too tight to wear, simple tops I never completed. Sticking with a project this huge was a deep challenge to my sense of self, seeing a task to completion. I had lots at stake trying hard not to ask, *Could this have all been a mistake?*

"I know," I said, as we tossed mud into the cement mixer, "let's pretend we're missionaries."

"Why?"

"It would give me a sense of higher purpose, as if we were sent here rather than *choosing* this punishment, this voluntary self-denial."

Lee went back to troweling mud onto the rising adobe wall of what would be our zome living room, only one adobe thick. We had decided early on to make our house two adobes thick, that is to say, twenty-four inches. It was like building two houses. Each adobe brick weighed forty pounds. My arms were like steel cables, my skin felt like burlap, and we hadn't begun the double-digit adobe walls yet.

The Thunderbird bar was more than a watering hole, it was a community center, a stagecoach stop for bewildered cowboys and stoned hippies. We'd taken to going there sometimes for a beer at the end of the day. Just being inside a cool dark place was a treat. Bars are comforting places for me. Once I walked from my home uptown in New Orleans all the way to Canal Street downtown walking into bars to catch the atmosphere, the music, the wonderful New Orleans accents that change block by block. But what made the Thunderbird so endearing was the mix of Anglos, Hispanics and Indians. It felt like the U.N. with a clock permanently stopped at 5:00. Sometimes we'd sit and eavesdrop in a booth, me mesmerized by the neon Coors waterfall that continually spilled, then recycled unnaturally blue glowing water. It was as lulling as a lava lamp.

A cone of light hung over the red cracked leather booths. A summer breeze and the light strobed and cast a jittery feeling. During the strong spring dust storms, however, it had an eerie swing to it, like a hangman's rope. Light leaked into the room from under the doors and from the dusty lights over the bar. There was a lost and found center, or as we called it, permanently lost center, on the top most shelves. The head of a doll stared at the pool table, a fake concho belt coiled next to the decapitated dolly, a frail, decaying snake skin of what appeared to be a rattler lay on its side and rocked slightly when the wind blew in. Sitting proudly like the portrait of a president was a giant picture of the mythical jackalope, the bar's official mascot.

I especially liked the calendar behind the bar that hadn't changed its date since 1968. I was told the young woman in the swimsuit with the jackhammer between her legs was related to someone in the bar who owned the body shop. Lee and I used to bet one another the same photo appeared month after month, but it was one of those ongoing bets we didn't care if we won or lost Each afternoon Angelo, the crosswalk guard from the elementary school across from the Thunderbird, appeared at 3:18. People set their watches to his arrival at his favorite barstool. Angelo's shoeshine black hair was coifed like a matador. Despite the fact he'd been accused of child molestation he'd had the job since he graduated from middle school.

The bartender Chuck had blurry tattoos of anchors on his beefy arm. He'd gone all the way through med school but when it came time to settle on a specialty the doctors told him he'd never be a physician with those tattoos. So he gave it up and started tending bar. Normally he spoke in such a soft voice you didn't know what he was saying, but once a thinly disguised developer in a bolo tie ambled into the bar. It was like a scene from a bad Western movie. I remember exchanging glances with Lee wondering if we were about to witness some kind of show down. The stranger in town didn't seem to know how to mount the barstool properly, propping his butt to the side, then swinging both legs in front of him as If he were in a swizzle chair in the barber shop. He made the mistake of piling his cards with the name of his Development, *The Aztec Way*, in a stack next to some drained beer mugs.

Chuck stared at the cards a moment then went back to his drying towel task. The developer flashed an overripe grin then asked for a martini, "stirred not shaken." There was just a moment's hush before the answer came: "Does this look like the kinda bar that serves James Bond drinks, pal? Does it?"

Dogs were regulars in the Thunderbird, so there was always the aroma of wet dog mixed with the yeasty scent of brew, cigarette smoke and, of course, the ubiquitous weed. Stalactites of fly paper hung near the doors. They were so overcrowded someone had written a small note on one: *no vacancy.* I never saw anyone put money in the juke-box that flashed like an alien's aircraft. But occasionally I would see a person reach behind the machine and push something. Someone fool-ishly tried to change some of the tunes on the jukebox, switching out Canned Heat for the more updated disco favorites that spun off from a new film., Saturday Night Fever There was such a furor, the account of "boo's" and "get outta here's" were followed by beer bottle throw-ing and even more serious threats. The guy was forever referred to as "Night Fever."

Downstairs, the space referred to as "The Underbird," had pool tables with scratch marks and dirty pool balls lined up side by side. In the comer was a playpen so dirty I can't imagine what might be breeding on the torn plastic mattress. A few broken trucks and a doll missing most of its hair made the nursery section complete. It was mostly kids that played around the pool tables, making kamikaze noises as they jettisoned the balls around the beaten surface. I once heard a rumor a baby was born on that table. Stories like that grew into fables with add-ons like "the big tree in the parking lot has the placenta planted beneath it. It grew double in one season."

For a while folks took turns cooking once a week... beans, mostly, and sometimes *posole*. This Thursday night all-you-can-eat-for-five-bucks event was popular during the winter months, but petered out in the summer when the main dishes turned out to be things like watermelon. Then the bathroom got really stinky with all the bladders already filled with beer; the tables extra sticky from the watermelon sugar

An unfortunate batch of stew sent folks running to the bathroom, some got as far as the parking lot. Esmerelda blamed Raphael, the cook that night, for carrying a batch of meat in the back of his pickup all day. It was later referred to as "Jim Jones goulash."

There was plenty of graffiti in the bathroom and next to the pay phone. Someone had written on the wall space next to the Ladies' Room "If You Live Outside the Law You Must Be Honest." This wisdom was attributed first to "Dylan Thomas." Someone scratched through that and wrote "Chairman Mao." Finally, at the bottom of the list was "Mama Cass, before the ham sandwich ate this."

Lee told me there was a sign next to the condom machine that read "don't eat this gum, it's terrible."

On the weekends it was live music at the Thunderbird, good stuff sometimes. Like the Halloween fol-de-rol featuring Bo Diddly who lived somewhere in the area. It was so dark in the bar, all the creativity spent on costumes was mostly lost to dim lighting. But the music was hot, and the floor was shaking.

At this time in the village's history there were many wounded vets from Viet Nam trying to put their psyches back together. We didn't know about Agent Orange. Perhaps the toxin's effects had been minimized. There were often a few guys thumbing around our area looking more lost than stoned, so dazed it was difficult to look into their faces.

But on that Halloween night, most of the confused young men

came out to party. It must have felt like a battlefield in there with the raucous guitar twanging and the drums firing off non-stop. The flickering lights and candle-lit pumpkins made the whole place feel underground. And then the lights went off completely. For about a minute the music stopped, but Bo Diddly continued on au Capella like the rest of us, used to power outages for no explainable reason. And so the band played on, unplugged which basically meant big drums and loud brass. With so much percussion, it nearly tore the roof off the place.

But a friend who had done two tours of Nam was sucked back into the rice paddies. He hit the floor thinking the place was under attack. It took us a while to understand just what had happened as he crawled underneath a table and relived the worst nightmares of his war life. But even with this post-traumatic stress happening before our eyes, most folks just kept dancing.

When we had the children with us, we'd let them romp in The Underbird a while, then get them French Fries and fizzy water. Morgan had an eye like an eagle, I grabbed a piece of tortilla out of his hand it was headed straight to his mouth. "Never eat anything from any floor," I told him, "especially this one." I was about to toss it in the garbage when I noticed "peace" was written on the tortilla in blue ink.

The bar sponsored "open mike" nights encouraging local and famous village poets, such as Robert Creeley and Gregory Corso to share their works. Our friend Larry was usually the main event, he was a first-class crowd pleaser in his outrageous outfits, upstaging the luminaries. My favorite getup was his muscleman suit, all fleshed out with preposterous abs, stitched together by his talented, artistic wife.

He often wrote his poems on tortillas and as a finale tore up the tortilla and tossed bits at the audience. Since Larry's last reading was given the previous month, it gave me an idea about the regularity of the cleaning service at the bar. That's the kind of bar it was.

We were sitting in the half light of the booth, Morgan stuffing fries into Lilah and eating crackers I'd brought. I thought the noise level was such that night that we could speak without being overheard.

"I wish we could just get some help for our building project." A set of heads turned our way as if I'd just mentioned this over a PA system in a school hallway. There were few jobs in our area and people were willing to do just about anything to subsist. If you wanted a decent wage, you had to go clear to Albuquerque and use a good portion of your salary on gasoline. Enterprising folks got into making jewelry, weaving; one guy made huaraches like the ones sold in Mexico with recycled tires for soles. Some, of course, sold drugs they'd home grown. But there was always the threat of the low flying planes surveying the hills for illegal crops. Jerry maintained that a place near Jemez called "Fervent Valley" grew the best dope in the U.S. "It's like Hawaii down there, man. Dig it."

The next day we heard a mumbly muffler, then saw a weather-beaten Volkswagen van chug down our road. I didn't think much of it; people we didn't know came and went looking for runaway teenagers or hoping to find a "crash pad" in the Free Form.

When the van pulled over, a tall young man climbed stiffly from the front seat, another pear-shaped fellow in overalls descended.

"Low," he addressed Lee. His eyes were intensely blue. He spoke as if he had a mouth filled with nails and screws. He had a disturbing Elmer Gantry look, an Evangelist looking for his lost flock. I had the urge to say, *Greetings, pilgrim.*

"Hello," Lee returned his greeting.

"Heard up at the Thunderbird you folks were looking for help."

"Zeke tell you that?"

"Nope, just floating around."

By then the rounder young man with curing shoulder-length hair sidled up. "I'm Jim," he said. "This is my brother, Dan. We tool leather."

"Thanks," Lee began, "but we don't need any leather goods. All of my slave driver whips are in fine shape."

This intended joke flattened and fell.

The fellow named Dan centered his gaze on Lee. "We were thinking we could barter work for a place to stay, use your water and camp out here."

Lee's face brightened. "Let's talk about this," he said.

Lee and I drove to North Fourth Street, looking in the mirror to make sure they were behind us. We lunched at a favorite spot not too far away: Sadie's Bowling Alley, best enchiladas in the North Valley.

They glistened in a pool of green chile sauce accompanied by doughy *sopapillas* deep fried ready to be filled with the honey that sat in a plastic container on each table. The guys were pretty straightforward: they would put in a few hours of labor daily in exchange for a place to set up camp. They'd use our water and electricity. We agreed to three hours of what they swore would be "committed" labor. Before I shook hands with them I wiped the excess honey from my hands. Just as we were sliding out of the booth Dan said, "Just one more thing."

"What's that?" Lee asked.

"We have another person living with us, my old lady Judith."

I shrugged. More female company might be enjoyable, so I nodded at Lee.

"She has some physical hang ups."

"By hang ups you mean?...Lee asked.

"She's got some kind of weird disease, can't move much."

"That's awful. What is it, like arthritis?"

"Dunno," he said. "It's tough." Dan turned his head back and forth. "So like we have to carry her everywhere."

"Has she seen a doctor?" I asked.

"She's a nature freak. Like she won't go near a regular doc."

"Do you have a wheelchair? How does she get around?" Lee asked.

"Wheelchair's man made. Can't go there. She likes being carried like the way they used to."

I immediately tried to put a timeline on *they* and *when*. The Civil War came to mind. Maybe she'd seen film clips of Viet Nam. I worried she might have something contagious. We had two small children. Dan seemed to read the hexagrams in my forehead.

"Chill," he said. "It's not catching."

How did he know that, I wondered.

"Where is she now?" Lee asked.

"Sacked out in the back of the van." Dan grinned.

"Dith is really cool the way she deals with her stuff."

"In the van? In the parking lot? It's a hundred degrees out there in the shade." My question offended Dan, I could tell by the way he fingered his ponytail, yanking at the gray strands.

Outside the sun was blasting down, glancing off the cars. "Wouldn't it be better to carry her into air conditioning?" Lee nudged my foot under the table.

"Dith doesn't like going from hot to cold, throws her into imbalance."

Silence passed around the table like a breadbasket. "Like she says, it's *her* body.

She knows what it needs. You dig?"

Lee and I talked on the way home, the hot air blasting into our windows. I began. "It scares me the way they ditch her in the parking lot. People can die if they're stuck outside in this weather without water." I nodded at the Albuquerque Bank thermometer now reading 102 degrees.

"Even dogs get treated better than that," Lee replied. "But let's just see how it goes."

That night I dreamed about the frail and mysterious woman, Dith. In my first dream I saw a tube like the gizmos in pet stores wired to the exterior of the cage, a hamster or gerbil sucking on the lifeline to water. Dith, the melancholy maiden, pressed pale lips to the tube, her face radiating woe, her hand white and clinging. In the second dream all four of us were present on the mesa nailing together a coffin using up the plywood we'd intended for our bond beams. I often have premonitions. This wasn't a good sign.

Dan, Jim and Dith chugged up the road, casing the mesa for the best clump of junipers. After week one they hadn't completed more than three hours of work in toto. I had only small glimpses of Dith as we were working hard to get the walls up during the summer months, and then pour the bond beam that held the structure together. We mixed mortar, carried it to the wall, slopped the mud on the course of adobes then went back at it. It took hours to make the promenade around the perimeters of the house, the living room, the kitchen, the children's room now resembling a swimming pool thanks to the pro bono work done by Jerry and his stoned friends.

I looked up towards the van. A few weathered lawn chairs leaned against the junipers. I was actually glad to see something that reclined: "Dith."

Jim was nowhere to be seen, and down in the valley. Later I spotted Dith for the first time. Dan had her strapped to his back like a backpack. He appeared to be surveying the property. She was pale and freckled, as I'd imagined. Her hair was a reddish golden color that caught the sun. Lee and I stood watching the procession. We dubbed her "the golden invalid." Dan stopped once and adjusted the sombrero which had slipped off her head and onto her upper back.

I'm glad I saw this tender moment; they'd been on our property for over a week and so far my compassion had already begun to ebb. The day for the raising of the zome was on the calendar. At Zomeworks, the pieces were being cut and they didn't have extra storage space for all our panels. I had penciled down a date for the event, the hoisting of the zome, calling it "erection day." We talked about this event in front of our "workers" to gently remind them we had a task at hand.

We had a pattern to the rhythm of our work much like the Swiss cuckoo clock in my parent's home, which on the hour released a mechanized couple, a male in Lederhosen stiffly chopping wood and a female doing something domestic, like milking a cow. They disappeared into the clock's interior, presumably still working until they were called onto stage an hour later.

I was beginning to get resentful of our workers as I continued with my mechanized pattern and so far they had done nada. I decided I'd introduce myself to the golden invalid, bring her some herbal tea but when I went down there Dan put his fingers to his lips. "Resting."

"Wish *I* could," I said with a soupcon of malice. "It's not easy working in the fierce sun all day then going home and cooking a meal, taking care of my children who have been with a sitter all day. We *pay* for her services, by the way. Then I have to wash clothes and put them on a line. I wash about two hundred diapers a week, and if I don't get them off the line fast they dry hard like adobes and feel like cement on my children's tender skin."

His eyes wandered. "I can dig it," he replied then disappeared under the tarp he'd strung up over the junipers."

At least *you* have shelter," I said and left.

Dan showed up to work just as we were leaving that day. I thought it convenient he worked while we were gone and there was no way to compute his hours.

On the way home we had to brake for something huge. At first, I thought I'd seen a mountain lion. "What was *that?*" Lee said. We watched it lope towards the "Free Form." I think it's a mastiff from hell. That dog could eat our children. I think we'd better have a word with Jerry. Keep it fenced in.

At the Thunderbird that afternoon we were asking around about the mastodon that seemed to roam free on the mesa like the dogs in the Sherlock Holmes novel. The bartender swiped the space in front of us. "That's Leroy. Guard dog."

"What's he guarding?" Lee said.

One of those quiet moments settled around us as eye traffic said *red light* to the conversation. It took about a week to find out why Jerry needed protection. Before we'd bought our land a "maverick" from the village calling himself Ulysses Grant threw his hat into the political ring entering the election for a new governor. He entered the Santa Fe courthouse in full regalia, riding a stallion. I could imagine the hollow clip clop of the horse hooves on the stone steps and then on the marble floors.

He got lots of support for this stunt. Apparently, things were going pretty well for U.S.G. until he shot his wife to death. This brought mixed reviews from the village. The posse had been after him since and apparently everyone but us knew he was taking refuge in our community, sometimes at a commune way out on the mesa, sometimes in the janitor's closet in the elementary school. To the hippie population this was a great scavenger hunt, forget he'd just shot his wife. We put two and two together. He was obviously being protected from the law by LeRoy, the dog from hell. Goody. I felt so much safer.

"I am going to make contact with Dith," I proclaimed one day.
"How?"
"I'm going to bring her something to eat."
"Like what?" Lee asked turning onto our road.

"I don't know. A yak burger or something. But it isn't right for her to be holed up down there. At least I'm going to hand her a bottle of suntan lotion."

"Being natural, as she is," Lee said, "she most likely won't use it unless it's been extracted from some rare herb during a full moon.

I figured everybody could eat beans, and since we ate them on a regular basis, I added more to the pot and brought them down to her. Dan had just toted her up from the dry arroyo bed. He was gazing out at the mesas as I approached. "She digs looking at the mesas."

"Good. I brought her some lunch."

He looked at the plate of beans and brown rice, shrugged his shoulders and pointed towards their wikiup.

"Hi, Dith," I said. "I'm Alice. I had some extra beans and thought I'd share them with you. If you like."

"Far out." She lifted up to her elbows on the green boy scout sleeping bag, took a sip from a metal canteen then fell backwards. "The boys will like it," she said. "Thanks."

"You're not hungry?"

"I have to eat a special diet." She pointed to a bunch of old canisters.

"Special grains, protein powders, ground mushrooms and some cosmic energy stuff that comes from the bottom of a lake in the Andes." She seemed exhausted by this explanation and stared at a pin prick hole in the canvas above her. "A healer said I needed to eat a cross between Hebrew and Asian. Hard to find that stuff out West." She drew a circle in the dirt. "Has to be combined in special colors: yellow, (she pointed to some imaginary yellow thing), green, red. No whites on the same plate."

She was more or less eating a color wheel. I figured on a diet like that no wonder she was wraith-like and disturbingly pale. As Dan said, "it's her body. Dig?"

At dinner that night after the kids were bedded down I suggested we give 'the boys' specific tasks, like cleaning up at the end of the day hosing down the cement mixer and the wheel barrow, cleaning the trowels, gathering up work gloves and lining them along the wall so they were dry the next morning.

"This is the very least they can do," I said. "I also have a fear I even hate to think aloud. Well, actually two things."

Lee bit into his eggplant, took a sip of beer. "Spit it out."

"Okay. Number one what if her unknown disease is contagious?"

"What's number two?"

"She's so fragile, I'm afraid she'll die out there, and then we'll have all kinds of possibility for a lawsuit. With those guys we probably wouldn't know until they buried her on our land. The place would become a cemetery and we couldn't build our house there."

Next I had a horrible thought, "Now that I think of it, if they stay here long enough, they might evoke squatter's rights."

"Oh, that's all. Glad you haven't let your imagination run away with you."

"Imagination? I haven't read a book in eight months. I don't have much of a mind left. Between mud holes and muddy-looking diapers my life is like an old television show I used to see called something like Death Valley Days. My blood pressure goes up every time I see old Dan sitting under a juniper tooling leather." I crouched forward to imitate Dan's Gepetto stance. "And by the way, guess who comes calling now?"

Lee shrugged.

"Our knight in armor, Jerry. Yesterday he rolled an empty cable spool onto the property. I thought he was bringing it over for the kids to play with, but no. He'd set up a poker game. For all I know they play all night. They probably have put out the word we're a casino by now." I slammed my feet down in exasperation. "We *have* to think of some way to get rid of them or they will be like that donkey we pass every day on the road. I don't know if it's alive or stuffed, it never moves. Like Trigger. Did you know when Trigger died they stuffed him? They might even stuff Dith if she dies, turn her into some strange healing cult. After all we have a renegade killer down the hill guarded by LeRoy, neighbors who throw sticks of dynamite around just to see how the place ends up. I think we've made a huge mistake. Huge."

"You need to get some rest," he said. "Tomorrow I'll set some limits. I promise."

The next morning I felt guilty about my breakdown. A little exaggerated, true. But I was afraid Dith was going to wither before our eyes. Everything dries up so fast out on the mesa.

When we took walks at night, I'd pick up something that I thought was a stick and realize it could have been the desiccated leg of a coyote. At night we could see dog packs running along the land that still belonged to the Bureau of Land Management. Coyote cries were pretty common, but there was also the rumor that wolves were afoot.

"I'm bringing Dith a baby pool," I said as we got onto the highway going to the site. "I saw them at the Bernalillo Mercantile half price. At least if she expires I can rest knowing I tried to hydrate her, reconstitute her like freeze dried coffee or something."

And so I walked to their encampment carrying the plastic baby pool, bright with pictures of orange fish, seaweed and coral. I wondered if there might be a restriction in color for things she sat on as it was for what she ate. At least there was nothing white in the plastic fantasy scene.

Under the paisley bedspread Dan and Jim were tinkering with some piece of the motor to their van across the junipers. What looked like the guts of the car was spread out on a bedspread like surgical instruments.

"Problem?" I asked. Lee was walking behind me carrying the play pool.

"I keep hearing some kind of thumping sound," said Jim. "Like something rattling around in the motor. Something's loose, maybe a screw."

At this prompt I gave Lee a look thinking there was a screw loose, no question about that.

"Listen," he began, "do you remember our agreement about doing work here on a *regular* basis?"

"Can this wait, man?" Dan said in irritation. He wiped his cheek with his arm.

"We'll *absolutely* talk about this tomorrow. The summer's fading away and we have to get these adobes up. We're only up four tiers. We have to get the bond beam poured, the entire zome room up-- that roof goes up in *one* day."

"Far out."

"*You* don't get it," Lee said again. "The team from Zomeworks is going to come out on a specific date with scaffolding and a crew. The zome is cut into panels and we have to screw them all together like a Rubik's cube. *All done in one day.* We have to be ready, walls up. Every wall exactly plumb or the panels won't fit together."

"Hey. We tool leather. We know about precise stuff." Dan was getting in a huff. Lee put the baby pool down.

"Thanks, man," said Jim, eyeing the baby pool. "We've been needing a bath."

"I bought it for Dith," I said emphatically, no mistaking my kindergarten teacher warning.

On the way home that night we passed another neighborhood sprawl, Jerry's brother's home. This was the home of the curious donkey that never moved. If it was stuffed, why was it tethered and if it was alive how could it stand in one place day after day? Something weird was going on out here, I declared aloud.

Lee downshifted. "Think that donkey's on drugs?"

"No, but it just gave me a great idea."

"I'm afraid to ask," Lee said.

"What if we tell the boys we've seen odd lights hovering at night. With all the stuff about cattle mutilations in New Mexico and Colorado, we might unseat them with a jolt of fear." I felt thrilled with the idea. "We could say the "I don't know. The only thing this plan might bring is us being the centerfold in the *National Enquirer.*"

"Hey, I've always wanted fame." But I was determined to use rumor and innuendo.

The next day I sauntered down on the pretext of seeing how the baby pool was working out. Dan told me that Dith couldn't sit on plastic, but they enjoyed a cool tub as the sun set. *Oh, great ...another reason for them to stay.*

"Say, "I directed my question to Jim who seemed to be the lesser of the two IQ wise, "ever see any odd lights out here at night?"

"What kind of odd lights?"

I used my hands to show hovering, then gliding through the air.

"Like that. Sort of."

"Like aliens, you mean?"

"Well, we keep hearing about the cattle mutilations-no traces of footprints or car tracks. And the other thing," I leaned in closer, "however this is being done it is being done with exact precision, like I mean surgical."

"That's so far out," he said.

"You aren't worried being miles from nowhere out here... so unprotected?

Lee said with just a teaspoon of concern.

"Wait a minute, I got to show you something." He disappeared into his van and returned with a giant strap the size of a wrestler's belt. It had odd markings all over it and still smelled like the tanning solution they used for dying.

"What do these lines mean?"

"This is what I wear every night walking around the mesa hoping those aliens will land. I've been trying to crack a code since I was ten, find lines and drawings like in those old caves... something ancient that might bring them down."

"What are you going to do when they arrive?"

"Fuck man, talk about the cosmos, what else?"

"What else," I echoed.

It was bound to happen. Jerry deeply befriended our work crew, showing up with dope and talking to them when they should have been working. We didn't dare interrupt as we'd finally made up with Jerry and wanted to keep him on our good side. He still had bouts of "helpfulness" when he took too many drugs. After the hole digging incident, I didn't want to push our luck.

One day during lunch a big gray truck bumbled down the road. I didn't know the driver, but in the back was Jerry in his wool cap waving like the king of Carnival. Next to him was a girl named "Ghee." I'd met her at the bar. She ate so much garlic she smelled like little Italy and claimed it kept her healthy. She was one of the young girls who showed up in town in a neat shirt and trousers and quickly adapted to cut offs and gauzy tops that showed her natural blessing for all to see. One of the odd things I noticed about Jerry over the time we knew him, he didn't hit on "chicks."

Jerry had long-winded theories about everything, particularly construction. I overheard him talking to Dan about building.

"The groovy thing about building is that you can get an idea and blam, over a weekend you can have a totally new house. Screw building plans." He looked at our adobe walls. "All that stuff about sealing the joints. Who gives a shit about a leak or two? A roof is just a tent, man. You got to let go of the boundaries. Come down at sunset and watch my walls change colors. Man, it's explosive. Living jewelry."

"I can dig it," Dan replied.

"And see," Jerry gesticulated, "with dudes coming in with new ideas, you got to let them explore, have their own plan, see where it goes."

I wasn't too thrilled to have him expound with someone who might take to adding a new wing to our house. With Jerry's "explosive" theory we might find new dynamite holes where we'd intended a kitchen. But, as we figured, it was better to say less to all of them rather than spur on their "inventive natures."

The one time we brought the kids up to play on the land when Dan and Dith were there, Morgan managed to put a tin pail on Lilah's head and it got stuck. My poor daughter was pulling and struggling to get it off her head running around and banging her fists against the tin.

"Lilah," I said in his gravelly voice. "chill out." He rested a hand on her shoulder and slowly revealed a pair of tin snips she couldn't see but Morgan could. "He's cutting off her head!"

Lee scooped Morgan up and carried him away from the scene. Jerry spoke to Lilah in a low soothing voice like a doctor about to administer a shot. I don't know what he said, but he managed to get her cooled down enough to get the tin snips to the metal chin strap, cut it off and slip the bucket off her in what looked like one seamless movement. She blinked in the loud sun, then let loose with the kind of crying that made her gulp for air. I held her until she quieted down vowing to discipline Morgan in a way that would definitely get his attention.

At home we were washing up dishes having bathed and read to the kids. "That's the last time we bring the children up there while those lunatics are on the land."

Lee dried a dish. "But they didn't have anything to do with the bucket deal."

"I know. But they creep me out. And I still worry about Dith having something weird."

"I believe the weird thing with Dith is between her ears." Lee pointed to his head. "I know but having someone with an odd disorder calls up the days when my father used to go to the leper colony near Baton Rouge."

"He worked at Carville?

"He volunteered there sometimes. Every time he came home, I hid under the bed while he bellowed our names from the foot of the stairs demanding we come down and give him a kiss."

"It upsets you to talk about it, I can tell by your expression."

"I hated having to touch him. I was afraid I'd get leprosy and my fingers would drop off. I was sure his clothes were carrying the disease."

Lee looked at me with great compassion. ''Nothing weird about growing up in your house," he said hoping to change my mood. When humor didn't change things Lee brought up the present predicament on the work site.

"I guess the alien ploy didn't work," Lee said.

"They actually like the idea of aliens up there," I replied. "In fact he has a little welcome wagon outfit ready to greet them when they whoosh on down."

"What about an eviction notice?"

"I'd rather throw the I *Ching*. "

"Let's flip a coin. Heads you tell them to get packing."

But I already knew I wouldn't do that.

The next day we found Dan painting a sign, a large sign.

"Starting up a shop somewhere?" I asked.

"Yep. We're calling the leatherworks 'Danudith.'"

"And you're hanging out your shingle?"

Lee joined me as the letter N took form on the sign.

"Okay if we just prop it out on the road with an arrow to the property?"

Lee looked at the sign. "Do you mean *our* property?"

"Yep."

We exchanged glances and walked in another direction.

"No way," I said. "What's next? Shops, teepees sprouting all over our land? Out." "We'll never get them out and,..."

"What about Dith?" Lee added.

"Wait. I have an idea. Maybe they don't know about Jemez Hot Springs. We could convince them someone has been cured of something there... like really serious. The water's supposed to have healing qualities. Once they pack, we'll just say they can't return. As in *No Trespassing*, this means *YOU*."

I looked towards their spread of junk beside their van. They'd accumulated more paisley bedspreads everywhere, even set out benches. A campfire pit blackened the earth and they'd set up gallons of water in smudgy containers I recognized as belonging to the health food co-op. They even had something that looked like a solar enema bag rigged, presumably so Dith could shower. Car parts were here and there. Close by they'd used old crates for their makeshift kitchen. A white dish drainer was filled with mismatched cups and saucers, platters that looked oddly familiar to me. They aired their sleeping bags on top of the junipers. But what was new as of that week was an old school bus, "a real bargain," Dan said.

They'd spent some time decorating it with psychedelic drawings; love and peace were written in a scrawl which made me think they'd enlisted the expertise of kids from the commune. I shuddered wondering what would happen if they rented their own tents at bargain basement prices. In terms of the art world we might end up with a permanent installation.

"We never should have allowed them to dismantle that damned motor." Car parts intermingled with paraphernalia for their tool and dye trade and even in the desert air we could smell oil and stench from the cans of dark dye. I suddenly got what it was with Dith. She had been poisoned by the fumes from their tooling. But if I dared suggest such a thing, well documented about dye, I feared one of them might draw a knife.

Lee marched back to them looking like Matt Dillon from *Gunsmoke.*

"Listen you guys, we refuse to have a nomad encampment on our land. Period."

Dan set down his paint brush, rubbed oil into a leather belt as if he hadn't heard a word. Two minutes later he turned his hurt, affronted look I in our direction, his eyes like two disappointed raisins in a pile of dough.

"See," Dan began. "That's what happens when people own property. They get greedy, like you folks. Can't share the bounty. Can't see beyond their personal needs. But hey, no problem." He drew in a breath for part two of his sermon. "But don't worry about us. We always make out, whatever life tosses at us, we're easy. Time for us to go North anyway. Communes in Colorado thrive on good will."

Jim had begun rolling up the tools in a piece of dirty cloth. Dith was collapsed on the dismantled front seat under a juniper, the one they'd removed from their now defunct van. Her arm lifted slightly.

We returned that night to see if they'd decamped. Signs that the caravan was pressing North were evident: some tents were down and half of the engine had gone somewhere, presumably back in the van. The lawn chairs had disappeared. Dith was nowhere in sight

The next morning, we took stock of our equipment. During the night, probably after dark, they confused our trowels, measuring tape, rebar, hammer and stain for their motor parts. That's the way we rationalized the missing tools.

Before the walls went up in the zome, we had to reckon with the fireplace. The proportions of a fireplace are crucial to its efficiency. We were after a kiva-type fireplace with a rounded exterior. It needs a damper, we discovered, or we'd be stoking wood like the folks on the Titanic. Now we were in a field we knew nothing about. Such words as flue, firebox, smoke shelf, and fire bricks were as unfamiliar as surgical procedures.

Although Jerry said he knew a dude, an Indian, who hung out at the merc. who was an expert on fire places. "The dude never uses any Anglo tools, he just eyeballs everything. I'll call him."

"Nope," Lee said so quickly Jerry shook his head in deep disappointment.

It was time to call in the mason/surgeon to get it right. We would learn from him, then the other fireplaces throughout the house would be our undertaking. And so while the masons began the arch, the interior form of our fireplace we were actually laying adobe bricks. One by one by one.

Since we were now using Zeke's adobes, we wanted the mortar we were mixing to match the quality of the bricks. The bricks can have some extra stuff like straw, an occasional pebble and so on. But any flaw in the mortar had huge consequences, Zeke told us, because any uneven mortar and the wall takes on a wonky look. Zeke told us to use trowels to make the mortar even. The smoothing over the layer of mortar with a trowel is an instant rock detector. You have to flick the interloper out and pour in more mortar. This wasn't going as quickly as I thought it might. But it was going.

The fireplace mason worked slowly, but efficiently, while we were in a road runner hurry to see results. We were constructing an arch in line with the fireplace. The idea was to be able to see through three arches from the kitchen clear to the zome. I called it the Scheherazade effect, each arch beckoning a person deeper into the story of our house. A wheelbarrow of mortar didn't last long, I discovered as I ferried it over to the zome. I'd decided if I wanted to have hands that didn't look like stucco, I'd better wear gloves. Just as a reminder of my toil, I kept tally of my efforts by hanging the worn gloves on a juniper. For some reason I thought about growing up in the south, the way dead snakes were left to dangle on wire fences until the sun set when they finally stopped their wriggling. I counted ten pair of gloves, all the fingers worn through. Sometimes as I trawled the mortar onto the wall I glanced over to them. They seemed to be waving.

Adobes are always stacked on edge, never flat. The chipped corners gave them the look of authenticity. But the best part of stacking them was they gave the illusion that a wall was already built. I looked for any sign of hope I could find.

We hadn't experienced many miracles (milagros) in our building life, so when the zome went up in one long day, I started thanking every deity I could claim from Zeus down to the Madonna. Mary is such a part of the culture we'd grown up in, it was an easy slide to see statues of her everywhere in the little villages nearby. The roadside shrines were particularly endearing, crowded with plastic flowers and small prayers, handwritten. I didn't know until I'd lived in New Mexico for a year that the descansos marked tragic car accidents.

I'd begun to think of the mesas that led to the feet of the Sandias I referred to as Zeus' throne room-their curves and drops, the footprint of a glacier melting. Little by little I was growing to love the heroic simplicity of the desert. As the cooler weather began to show up, I could watch the shadows float over the mountains. I was finally a Southerner who stopped looking for trees, comfort and security. Each rain sprouted the mesas, a crew cut of bright green appeared like a kid's science project, or the ceramic lambs sold in Old Town that, when watered, sprouted green hair.

I began to appreciate the trees and shrubs that were around me, as well. The Russian olives with their narrow silvery leaves, the fluttery disc-like leaves of the cottonwoods, the *pinon* with its nutty fragrance, the Catalbas with leaves big enough to cover our children's head and, finally, the Tamarisk with its shaggy bark and fine, feathery foliage that flushed pink in early summer. Embracing so much nothing, as the desert presented, was an act of faith. But first, I realized, /had to shift my vision. I'd found a quote by Emerson I kept on the windowsill: "The health of the eye seems to demand a horizon. We are never tired, so long as we can see far enough."

I decided to train my eyes on the mesas in the Jemez mountains, also that same day an old friend from New Orleans drove up. Milagro, help was on the way, his name was Johnny, just in time for the zome to go up. He lived with us for the next year, working on the house for room and board.

I always called that day Erection Day. First the Zomeworks folks arrived with extra friends, their families, and children to watch this event. We were like the state fair for one day. But it was a long, tense day. If our adobe walls were off even slightly the whole project would have to be ditched like a failed space shot. Weeks before the zome went up, we'd poured a cement bond beam around the top of the structure. We'd put bolts in strategic places for fastening the panels.

On the day of the zome construction, other friends showed up for the barn raising the usual crowd from the bar who liked to sit on stacks of adobes, drink beer and make suggestions, much like the people who watch skyscrapers go up in a big city.

First scaffolding had to be fit together, then the structure went up like an erector set, once the rebar was in it was accumulation, screwing and hammering.

Morgan was delighted as the metal scaffolding stood in the center of the zome, as if this giant jungle gym were there for his pleasure.

As the team stacked the zome panels against the adobe walls, Morgan swung from the bars like a chimp, annoying some of the guys who weren't children friendly. Lilah squirmed out of my arms to get to her brother and the playground he'd made of the zome.

We had to hang a rope in the center of the dome and Lee was going to use it to seal silicon in all the spaces between the panels once the whole thing was done, we'd paint the panels a dark oxide red color. The panels were fastened to the bolts leaving an open space along the first layer we would fill with adobes so the entire zome had an earthen quality.

We also had decided to suspend a loft on the wall facing the mesas. It was attached by steel poles. Once the loft was in, voila, we had a guest room. We just needed a ladder. From the loft we could see even farther into the mesas towards the extinct volcano Cabezon, and the blue range of Mount Taylor.

"This is an elevating event," I told one of the workers, "the only thing that's happened so far like clockwork." The gang from Zomeworks worked like a team of surgeons as they moved the scaffolding around the adobe structure, clanging and constructing deconstructing the tall pipes and boards they used for standing. I was so thrilled that day, I would have likely been happy to just throw a tarp over the scaffolding and call that our living room. A structure along those lines would have made Jerry happy. Jerry, I noticed, didn't show up until the end of the day when we were passing out beer by way of a celebration. It was as if he'd planned the entire thing himself.

"Dude," he sidled up to one of the Zomeworks guys he knew. "View's far out." "Literally," said Jake as they both gazed at the Jemez Mountains across the mesas.

I wondered if Jerry would address the other architectural aspects of our growing house, the four sides and roof he once called "A Taco Bell," but he generously stayed with the beauty of the zome's structure. He gave us his greatest blessing: "Cool." But as we knew his scavenger nature we figured he was there to scalp up anything not nailed down. Jerry and his buddies enjoyed nothing better than taking a sledgehammer or a crowbar to an abandoned building and pulling out copper wires, pipes to anything he could recycle. I kept an eye on his movements during the day.

Meanwhile the panels began to unite, hammering rang through the room, the sweet sound of echo. The sound of a shelter. I didn't want anyone to know that for the past few months I'd been dreaming about living in a prefab house with green Astroturf and a stuffed donkey in the front yard.

The panels climbed and then the fine moment of handing up a small stained window we'd designed: an Arabic star, vermillion, green and cobalt blue, designed by us, handcrafted by a German who brought the glass from Munich. Once in place it became a focal point with sunlight providing the drama as the backdrop.

The poles that suspended the loft were in place. That was done last. From the loft we'd left several panels open to be glassed in for a momentous view of the mesas, Cabezon and the Jemez Mountains. I couldn't wait for the end of the day when we could hoist a ladder up to the loft and watch the sunset from that elevated point. It was like having an observatory for a living room.

Progress looked so beautiful. We all applauded as the last panel got screwed into place, the loft hung. A low wind whistled through the glassless giant windows facing the Sandias. We were finally alone in time for the sunset. A roof over our head, the ghostly sound of the flapping plastic sheets covering the stack of adobes.

With the shelter of the zome we had a sense of protection, could bring the children to the site where they played in the dirt that was the floor of the living room. It was a comfort to have the family gathered, have picnics for lunch and sometimes dinner as well. But then, of course, we had the rest of the house to build.

In the shank of that afternoon we spread an Indian bedspread on the dirt under the zome enjoying the quietude. The children seemed to catch our sacred moment, lying down next to us.

"What color is that window?" I pointed to our beautiful new cobalt blue window. "Blue," Morgan said with enthusiasm.

"What is that hanging from the ceiling?" "A loft," Morgan said.

I took Lilah's hand and pointed to the *Sandias*. "What do you call those?" "Mountains," she said proudly.

"What's that?" I pointed to clouds bunching over the *Sandias*. "Clouds."

"What do you call this whole place?" I made a circular replica of the zome with my finger.

"Our house," she jumped in beating her brother out of an answer that made me feel so good I had to turn my head away to hide my tears.

Later that afternoon when the sun was low enough to make long shadows, we walked down through the crunchy sand of the arroyo to see what our house looked like from below. I remember Morgan stopping to look closely at a cactus growing by the side of the road. He often did that on our walks as if he were going to go back home and draw the plant from memory. Lilah liked walking between Lee and me so we could stop occasionally and swing her up in the air. Our little lion lady, as we called her, wanted to fly.

I spent much time on Fourth Street driving to the hardware store we used for buying supplies. I figured we'd given them thousands of dollars in trowels and gloves, rebar and cement. We didn't have contractor's prices, and we had to buy enormous quantities of cement bags at top dollar. We were forever going through tubes of silicone sealant, as all the panels in the zome needed to be closed against leaks. I kept the receipts. It wasn't hard to guess how much the hardware store was adding onto the wholesale prices, probably doubling the price. I compared them to the bags I saw being bought by friends who knew contractors. In the parlance, we were being ripped off big time.

On days designated as errand days the kids would pile into the Scout and we'd drive through the Rio Grande valley towards the hardware store and co-op. On such occasions I would tell them how it was growing up in New Orleans where they still had French and Creole words like *banquette* in use. I described the Cajun canoe that snaked through the marshes called a *pirogue,* only about an inch from the water. I told them about the Creole custom called lagniappe, where a child would be given a surprise from the owner of grocery store.

"Like what?" Lilah's attention sharpened.

"Usually licorice, or maybe peppermint."

"I thought you didn't think we should eat candy."

I thumped the steering wheel. "That was then. This is now."

It was just by accident I discovered I *could* get cement and sealant at wholesale prices. It was a hot day, hotter than usual and I was buzzing along waving to familiar faces in our building world who sold us our doors, windows and odd things we needed for an authentic look in our house. Looking straight ahead I passed the flea market, finally pulling into the hardware store. I'd been working all morning, so I had on my short cut-off jeans and a halter top. I didn't normally go around in abbreviated clothing as I got stared at enough just for being so blonde. I went into the store to pay for cement. The clerk, a hippie named Jasper, loaded it on off the dock in the back of the store.

"This mark-up is an outrage," I commented, as I wrote out yet another check. "Yep. And if you knew what piss poor wages I get, you'd be even madder... that sucker is a millionaire practically."

I figured."

I noticed he was giving me the eye as I shifted from one foot to the next writing down the amount of the bags. We could only haul so many bags in our Scout. Even then, the car dragged along the road and sometimes if l made a turn too quickly, it fish tailed.

That day I was watching Jasper load up the cement bags. Ten was about our limit. I counted to ten, then noticed him smiling as he tossed on an extra two bags. "Compliments of the scum bag," he said, giving me a big wave.

Who was I to complain? This was just good old Southern *lagniappe*.

Sometimes wearing abbreviated bait shorts and a skimpy top worked against me. When I told Lee about the afternoon he suggested I keep that outfit in the back of the car for any forays to the hardware store.

"Pimp," I said.

He winked at me and smiled.

Finally, we were in our third trimester; we'd see those babies go up and form a wall. Adobe by adobe. Anyone coming to visit us that summer was put to work. Our steadfast friend Johnny ended up living in our Corrales house until the overwhelming movement our toddlers drove him to quieter places. Ginger, an old New Orleans friend, helped on the weekends. We had window frames made. After four courses of adobe layers, we set the window frames and saw, for the first time, the view we'd be seeing from our kitchen. From this window on the world we could be anywhere: Morocco, West Africa, Timbuktu. I wouldn't have been surprised to see loping camels. I touched the walls, felt the rough texture of our home, its harsh resilience, and understood for one brief moment the solitude of the desert. Four layers. For some delusional reason I thought we were halfway there.

When the walls were up to eight feet high, I realized that lifting forty-pound adobes over my head was something weight lifters did, but doing it on a metronomic basis was too much challenge for me. Several friends commented on the wall I was constructing that led into our zome living room. First they'd look, up, down, then lapse into silence.

"What?" I asked.

One person pointed to the wall. "It bulges, looks like it might have been rammed by an iceberg." I was miffed. This house was my confidence building PhD, and I was really proud that I could see it happen. Well, maybe it bulged just a *little* bit. I thought about how much damage one pebble in the mud layers could cause. I knew my walls weren't exactly "plumb" but somehow that didn't have larger implications until I saw the wall towering. Plumb. One small thing, a rock, and the whole place could crumble. It was a large metaphor for life, I figured standing before my wall, knowing it would be impossible to repair at this stage. All the adobes would have to come down, and the connecting walls that were now tied in. I could hear my father chastising me for being sloppy. He was a surgeon and often had temper tantrums in the operating room ending up with him throwing all the scalpels and equipment for the surgery across the room sending the nurses scurrying. Actually, one of his tantrums would have been useful if it involved pitching a few adobes into place. Ironically the bulge in my wall was Jerry's favorite point of interest. *"No* wall should be plumb," he told me. "Plumb isn't organic."

What a difference between us, my father and me. His life was all about order. As I looked at trowels, overturned wheelbarrow, gloves tossed on adobe piles, I realized my life invited chaos. My father would often come into our bathroom to see if we'd put the top on the tube of toothpaste. He was like a boot camp sergeant.

Once he rubbed the open tube of paste against my gums until they bled, a reminder to cap the thing. I didn't do that again.

Having a wall come down because I had miscalculated was one of those incidents that brought up warnings from childhood, the kind teachers used as threats when I was in school: *This* will go into your *permanent* record. I remember at my high school graduation listening to a boring speech, wondering where my permanent record was stored now? Did I have time between the end of the graduation ceremony and the prom to sneak into the school's archives and destroy my permanent record? What had those mean-spirited teachers put in there anyway? Your *permanent* record indicates there was a pebble in that mud, that you went ahead and laid the adobes on top anyway. Your carelessness will cause havoc in the future. If not to your family, to those that follow. Maybe not in your time, but some time. These were my punishing thoughts as I looked at the wall, I would have to pass every day, wondering if my time was coming.

It isn't good to lay more than six or seven courses of adobe in one stretch; they need a little time to settle like a cake. We were so tired halfway through the day we'd both quit using a plumb line to see if the walls were straight. Knowing that Lee was also cutting corners, so to speak, somehow reassured me. If another wall came down in a different location, I could talk to him about *his* permanent record.

We were told to use something called a "story pole" to remind us about the dimensions of the windows. There was something thrilling about seeing a framed window. Our territorial windows facing the mesas had a direct view of the extinct volcano, Cabezon.

These windows facing the mesas from the kitchen were handmade and set into the adobe, structures so heavy it took four guys to lift them in place, made by a wonderful carpenter named Locendo Lesperance. Dr. Menge had given us his name after we'd complimented the details of his Corrales territorial style adobe. Setting views into place, framing the vista with gigantic portals to the universe was, next to the erection of the zome, the most thrilling of moments, letting us know we had caught the right moment in the frozen music of our construction. And now we had two spectacular views, the gigantic window in the zome facing the Sandias as well as the territorial view of the mesas. We congratulated ourselves, puffed with pride at our good choices. Still, we had so far to go.

Every day I had to tell myself we weren't really crazy to be taking on this task. But we needed help. I was eating aspirin every night for my back ache. I felt as if my bones were leeching into the desert floor. Pretty soon I would resemble the hunch back flute player called Kokopeli, a motif that shows up all over the Southwest. I was beginning to understand the language of cave painting in a visceral way.

This time we called on Zeke for workers rather than consult the grapevine that strangled the Thunderbird Bar gossip network. Before long two men showed up: Librano and Jose. Librano was all smiles; Jose quiet, reflective. Librano dressed in bright shirts covered by a soiled pea coat; Jose was clad in Johnny Cash black complete with pointed cowboy boots, a dark moustache. They were not only steady hard workers, they were wonderful with the children and talked to them in Spanish, played ball with Morgan, sang to Lilah. They were adept. I loved stepping back between batches of mud mortar I'd wheeled over and watching their circus-like maneuvers. I handed a shovel of mud from the wheelbarrow to Librano, he tossed the entire shovel up to Jose who troweled it flat. They never spilled a drop-the movement was weightless, balanced.

Their show was like something I'd seen under the big top where the impossible seems light, airy and completely do-able. And their steady moving hands kept us working harder, just to keep pace with them. I have no idea where the stereotype of "lazy Mexican" sleeping under a sombrero came from. From our experience it could not have been farther from the truth.

Working along with Jose and Librano was like taking an art course. Jose could trowel the perfect amount of mud onto the wall, run the trowel down and have no drippy excess like the messy icing I'd been working on. My swollen wall distressed both of them with its middle age kettle-like bulge. The only comment was a tsk, tsk, tsk from Librano, then he sucked air through his teeth. I asked in my best Spanish how to repair this mistake; he shrugged his shoulders. I figured with their expertise the walls would be corrected somehow.

Since Jose and Librano didn't own a vehicle, we drove them back and forth to their separate dwellings on the outskirts of the small town of Bemallilo. Jose lived with a woman in a white trailer and her brain-damaged son, Benjy. Out back, I spied a smaller trailer that looked like an iron lung with a window and door. My first guess was this was a hold out for men like Jose who needed a bed and a bath, but were not staying long.

The first time I met Jose's "amiga" I was amazed with her dancing blue eyes, her orange cotton candy hair, her gingham apron and her cowboy boots. Jose met her, she explained, when her car had rolled over an arroyo and she was hanging upside down, hoping someone would drive up, hopefully not the law. "Never wish to see the sheriff out here," she said, then added, "and especially the INS." She nodded her head towards Jose. There weren't many words Jose knew in English, but he sure knew the word immigration. I introduced myself to this woman who called herself, "The Minority of One."

"After all," she said wiping her hand on her apron, "who's gonna want to shack up with a wetback?"

I was pretty amazed she used this derogatory term within earshot of Jose, but he kept a smile on his face. They were *braceros,* a term meaning Mexicans with strong arms who show up and do what no one else will. I thought that term less offensive, somehow. But there was no doubt as to their land of origin. Using the term *braceros* was ubiquitous.

"He built that tin shed out back," she pointed to a utility shed with room enough for a large mower if anyone ever needed such a thing in the South West. "Good with the kid, too." Jose was teaching Benjy carpenter skills so he could find a job. Benjy appeared to be about thirteen. He was a sweet kid who periodically took off his hat and hit it across his knees. Like Jose, his hat was black and my guess was he'd chosen it to mirror his hero.

"Sometimes Jose takes us with him to the wrestling matches," she told me. "Problem with that is the Immigration folks know that's a watering hole for wetbacks, so they sometimes spring a surprise visit and round them all up. He's been back and forth three times this year."

I wondered if Jose was paying rent. Their housing relationship was clear on one level; Jose was muscular and tanned and if he could handle a woman like he handled mud and mortar, she was a happy lady. I knew he sent money to his family in Mexico because we'd arrange money orders for him to send down to Chihuahua.

Librano's Bernalillo family was all Hispanic. The woman's name was Mrs. Perez and she had at least three children, maybe they were grandchildren, and an ancient crone of a grandmother all smushed into their small adobe. A seven-year-old named Inez always came running when we drove up. She danced around him and jumped up and down until on corn and sugar.

On Sundays the entire Perez clan joined us on the land to picnic. Loud music crackled from a portable radio and the kids climbed all over the ladders, getting Morgan and Lilah to join them in their calisthenics. Meanwhile we watched the shawled, elderly grandmother scamper down the hillside. Sometimes she was gone for as many as two hours. I figured she wasn't sunning herself down there, but I was surprised when she appeared with armfuls of what looked like weeds, *chamisa* and unidentifiable brush. Mrs. Perez explained that her mother was a *curandera,* made *tonicos* with those herbs and sold them in the Bernalillo Mercantile. The old woman was amazingly limber, thrashing away at the weeds with a machete, cutting off that stuff that she didn't need and bundling them up, always smiling and calling to the children. All the while blaring horns and Mexican music broke the silence of our home. After they ate a large lunch of homemade tortillas, beans and some red meat I now know, as *carne adovado,* they'd stretch out for an hour's siesta, in the zome, some in the car. It all depended on how many showed up that day. And so we got in the habit of leaving them at peace for their Sunday afternoons after lunch. I never worried about any of our tools going missing.

At last I got to play with the children more with this added help. Morgan would often stir the mud in the wheelbarrow before Librano tossed the shovel towards Jose. Both guys were wonderfully patient when the children interrupted such a task, pulling back and allowing them to explore the world of building. Unlike our former helpers, Jose and Librano allowed all of us to relax a bit. They had no time table. The day's work was over when the sun went down. I remember seeing their silhouettes against the rising walls, admiring Jose's stiff posture. He could have been a star in a Mexican film. And they were vigilant about cleaning up, hosing down the tools, sometimes giving the kids a squirt.

Their presence allowed me to spend time with the children in the zome reading stories after lunch, *siesta* time. I remember having to dust off the library books before I returned them to the Bernalillo library. Morgan had a penchant for Richard Scary with all of the busy things people did all day. Lilah was more drawn to the stories of a badger named Frances who had a tough disposition. Whoever dreamed up this funny little character knew children like our daughter. The author designed ways to honor a child who maneuvered the world (even at her early age) with logic.

Once, years later, an elderly friend of Lee's grandmother invited the children out to lunch. I was suddenly worried about their manners. Not basics like *please* and *thank you,* but using a napkin properly and wiping their mouths. Mrs. Mahoney told Lilah if she ordered a large plate with a hamburger and fries she would be obliged to eat it all.

And Lilah agreed. But she ate only half of her meal. Mrs. Mahoney reported that when she reminded Lilah of their agreement, she replied, "Yes, Mrs. Mahoney. I said I'd eat it. But I didn't say when and I didn't say where." I loved Lilah's mind, so distressingly acute like her father's.

My next house task was to skin the *latillas,* aspen poles, that would be the under layer of our ceiling, wood planks going on top of that. I remember taking a drawing knife and peeling the bark off long aspen poles. *Latillas* are usually laid between the beams, or *vigas* in a herringbone pattern. It is a labor-intensive job I learned fairly quickly. Once I found the rhythm of a task, I could perform it more efficiently like learning to play something on the piano, the metronome ticking. Skinning latillas was like rowing, and had a pleasant cadence to it, until the end of the day when my back began to hurt. The ceiling above the latillas would be all wood, with insulation poured, or in our case, foamed on top of that.

The peeled bark of the aspens curled in a circle around me. Morgan wound the peelings around his baby sister's head, made a wreathe for her, then turned the remaining bark into a long "choo choo" train, pulling it through the dirt, making sounds that seem to be part of little boys' DNA no matter what language they speak. I was beginning to worry he would be like that cartoon character named Gerald McBoing-Boing who only made car noises, beeped, honked and generally did a good imitation of the freeway. And so I began to take more time out reading to them, toting book bags up to the land, sitting on the dirty floor listening to the sound of wind through juniper branches, the cranking sound of the cement mixer.

While I worked, I told them stories about how mountains are made. I astonished them by telling them that fossils of sharks had once been found in the walls of the Grand Canyon. As I told them, they drew pictures of sea creatures swimming in the deep caverns, crabs climbing up the walls of the place, beach umbrellas spread on the canyon's rim for the pleasure of the tourists. They liked the mysterious story about the tribe of Indians who disappeared off the face of the earth: the Anasazi. They made up stories about what might have become of them. Eaten by coyotes? Cooked by other Indians?

Maybe they learned to fly. I liked that one best. On weekends we drove up through the Sandias and had picnics by a stream. It was cool up there, shaded and smelled of trees and water. It brought me so much joy to have a gurgle factor back in my life.

The theory is this: when your walls are up, the roof is on, you are half done. We were bumping up against cool weather, coming short of adobes, and we joined the long line of builders like us, caught short in the startling realization there was a seasonal aspect of building with adobe. Where had the time gone? Zeke promised us two hundred adobes, at a price that was just short of usury. We had few choices. When he didn't show up with our promised bricks we started asking around. We finally found him at Anita's Restaurant where he was enjoying a huge chile burger and a beer with some guy with a New York accent. Lee walked over to him. Zeke put his burger down, sipped his beer.

"Zeke, we can't go any further until you deliver those adobes. We have to get the bond beam poured before cold weather sets in."

Zeke worked at something in the back of his mouth with a toothpick.

The guy with the annoying Brooklyn accent broke the silence. "He just sold me his last three hundred adobes."

"Wait a minute." Lee's face got red. "They were sold to us, and for a lot of money."

The guy, a famous New York photographer named Danny, laughed. "I'd sell my own mother out for those adobes, Bud. They're mine now." The way he said mother sounded like *Mu-tha*.

"Zeke. What kind of deal is this?"

"A money deal, Johnson. He paid more."

"But you promised them to us.

"You forget something, Johnson. You didn't pay for the whole thing." He rubbed his second finger and thumb together as if caressing a hundred-dollar bill.

Lee leaned in closer to make eye contact with Zeke. "You can't do that. A deal's a deal. Give me my money back, you just can't do that."

"Well, Johnson," he said slowly, "I just did."

Lee was so mad he couldn't speak. He kept looking over at the guy who'd so gleefully messed us up.

"Asshole," Lee said loud enough for him to hear.

And so we were out looking for adobes at the last minute, knowing we were competing with everyone in the entire state. In a week the state fair would open and it would be impossible to get hold of anyone.

It was time to visit LoLo, the true purveyor of goods, ill-gotten and otherwise.

Old man LoLo was a courtly gent. His khaki pants and shirt were always ironed, and he sported a fedora hat. His white moustache had a Salvadore Dali edge, but he was all quiet respect.

Not only did old man LoLo find some bricks for us, he also managed to find the mythical bridge timbers we wanted for our ceiling, old beams from a crumbling hacienda in Espanola, and finally the weathered ties we laid across the bond beam once it was dried. I don't know how he got the bridge and who might be standing at the edge of a dry arroyo wondering how he or she would get across without the wooden planks that were now missing. Ever since the run-in with the New York celebrity photographer willing to sell his mother, I'd began to look at "deals" in a new way, willing to ignore some obvious signs of skullduggery. Was I compromising my values? Sure. When in Rome.

Better than the bridge timbers he delivered, Old man LoLo also showed up one day with the most beautiful *vigas* I'd ever seen. As it turns out, they came from Santo Domingo pueblo from a house probably a hundred years old. The extra touch was the carved opening at the end of each *viga* for hanging meat or *ristras*. Ristras are to New Mexico what garlic strings are to Italians. *Ristras* are strings of red chile, now an obligatory decoration to anyone wanting the "southwestern" motif. And *ristras* are as functional as the strings of garlic. Grab a few and grind them into powder, essential for dishes like *carne adovado.* Warning: wash your hands after peeling chile. Our term for not remembering to do so was "attencion: zi zi picante."

While we lived in New Mexico we tasted every level of chile. Reportedly the best chile comes from a place called Hatch. If you don't like chile, you are immediately suspect. It will cure what ails you, especially known for taking care of the common cold due to its high Vitamin C content. In our favorite restaurant in Bernalillo, the hamburgers were served with chile. Our children ate chile on everything, passed the New Mexican test of valor at Anita's Restaurant by not flinching when they served the kids the hottest chile, *serranos*. Even McDonald's caught on and featured chile burgers. We learned to blister green chiles on the stove, peel them and put them on everything.

Posole, a dish I associate with Christmas and potluck meals, is loaded with green chile. *Bueno Chile* in a container looking like margarine, was a staple in our refrigerator, it comes frozen or fresh. I still miss chile on just about everything.

One day I was mixing mud when I heard a creaking sound. Not the creaking of wheelbarrow, or any wheel, in fact. This was the sound of someone putting on gigantic shoes. Then there was a horrendous rush of air, a blast. There was nothing around me. It took the gigantic shadow to make me look up. It was a runaway airborne circus, brightly striped hot air balloon drifting in the sky like a child's fantasy. I made a dreadful mistake by rushing the children outside to see the whimsical beast that dominated our back yard. Morgan was nearly beside himself with excitement. Lilah, wrapped in my arms, stared at this odd visitor. We waved and yelled. The balloon began to descend, leaving an exhaust of fumes and noise that I associated with a dragon. He got close enough to call to us. I recognized immediately from his accent he was German. The balloon was now so low we could call back to one another. It was either dropping down completely or waiting for an updraft to return it to the sky. In any case, Morgan ran towards it. "Morgan," I yelled. The balloonist smiled and called back "Morgan!" Translated into German, *Morgan* means morning. As in, Good Morning! This call and refrain went on as the balloon came closer, and Morgan was within reach of the gondola's sand bags and drifting ropes, the ones that tethered the balloon to earth. Before I could stop him, Morgan had grabbed hold of one of the ties. Soon he was treading air.

"Lee, Jesus, help me," I called. The balloonist's face went white. "Get away little boy." But, like many people, he saw a large little boy who was just barely two and mistook him for an older child. An older child who could speak. "Get away," the man kept screaming over the sound of the rushing air. Lee got to Morgan and grabbed hold of him around the middle shaking his arm so he was forced to drop the tie from the balloon.

With a whoosh, it lifted off, wafting towards the Sandia Mountains, the man shaking his head, occasionally covering his eyes and probably wondering why American children were so undisciplined.

After lunch that day we sat down, Lilah in my lap and Morgan straddling a pile of adobes, riding them like a horse.

"Listen, Morgan, Lee said in his stern father voice. "That was very scary. Don't you ever do something like that again. You have to listen better."

Morgan paid little or no attention to Lee.

"Did you hear me? You could have been killed or dragged up the mountain side by that balloon. When we say *stop,* we *mean* it. Look at me when I'm talking to you."

Morgan glanced at Lee; returned to his galloping adobe.

"It's hopeless," Lee said, standing. "One day you are going to get hurt by being foolish like you were today."

I caught just a small glimpse on Lilah's face. It was the look of the sibling who didn't get into trouble. Her mind was a storage file gathering information on how to proceed by stepping out of harm's way and letting her brother step into it. Her wisdom was tinged with humor and irony.

I nudged Lee. Abstract threats, I knew, didn't work and they particularly didn't work with children who were super-charged with equal amounts of energy and curiosity.

Once visiting New Orleans my mother suggested we put the two of them on a leash. I found that idea barbaric. We'd moved to the desert, I told her, to open space, so they could explore the world without fear of on-coming cars.

"You still need to civilize those children," she replied. "That is your job."

Early on we'd decided we wanted mostly brick floors, with the exception of the zome living room. In that large space we settled on dried earth. I'd seen earthen floors in homes in Santa Fe and Corrales, never forgot the room in Dr. Menge's adobe hacienda.

They had a burnished, cracked look and felt wonderful to the naked foot.

In the 1800's, earthen floors were the natural choice for adobe homes due to the lack of saw mills. But it was the 1970's and we were still easily seduced by the weird and wondrous. We were like Toad in *Wind in the Willows*, swept away by whim and fancy, taking on the most difficult kind of flooring. Mud had to be poured about four inches thick, then dried. Then it cracked. The cracks had to be filled in. Then it dried again. Cracked. And so on but we were Moroccan-mosque-stricken again, our minds wandering back to kasbahs and souks. We *had* to use this natural flooring.

We went about gathering information from folks we'd met along our arduous journey who agreed, it was the most authentic look a person can have for floors. We learned of the Spanish custom: once the mud is poured, cracked and dried, an animal is butchered in the center, its blood filling up the tiny ravines. *No, thanks.*

I remember the discussion had at dinner. "I absolutely refuse to do that," I said.

"But did you *see* those floors, how beautiful?" Lee said.

"Sorry."

Once my father's weird idiosyncrasies became part of the arguing landscape, we were off and running. In my mind the many building voices echoed, *You may build the house, but you won 't stay married.* And we had been going at it for over a year over every house detail. Throwing my father's name into an argument was a diversionary tactic, I knew. It always worked. Got me off subject and into the haunted past.

Most folks referred to the heart of their family home as their living room. I called my living room *the interrogation room.* "Called down on the carpet" had a special meaning for me as I recalled the badgering sessions, me standing on our Persian rug tracing figures with my big toe as my father launched into one of his endless lectures about right and wrong, eventually steering towards the topic he could never forget: integration. I don't know why he thought his children were somehow responsible for this social change, but he felt in some way we had contributed to it.

Lee and I battled over window heights, spaces between beams, which lintel would go over which window and the thousands of ungodly decisions, the interminable lists that needed to be made on a daily basis. Sometimes we'd hold up a board to see where one of us thought the wall should end, the window begin. Often the disputed territory we fought over was only a few inches. During these unpleasant spats Jose and Librano would move into a shady spot, perhaps under a juniper, and play a game of cards. I know the kids hated these fights as well. I could tell by the way they got quiet and gave one another looks. Often they would sit down next to Jose and Librano until we'd come to some settlement. Neither of us are willing to give when it comes to aesthetics.

Jerry, I discovered during one of these quarrels, was like one of those tag-along folks in a museum tour who listens but doesn't want to pay the guide. He'd sometimes quietly step out from behind a juniper and offer Lee a toke. Of course, we knew he'd been getting the full gist of our fight. Sometimes he'd add his own commentary like "So you folks are pacifists?"

He was also listening when we discussed who would put the rough-ins for the wiring. Who would be our electrician, and could we trust Zeke ever again? What if we got somebody who was on drugs and wired the house so that no light switch matched the light in the room and we'd be forever trying to figure out how to turn off lights?

"I know this groovy dude," Jerry broke in and told us, "who can fix up your wires so you never get an electric bill. Never gets caught. Genius."

Rather than hear how "uptight" we were, fearing jail sentences for breaking the law and all, we ignored his helpful musings about our wiring concerns.

Some things we knew for sure. We knew for certain we were going to have mud floors in the zome room, agreed to pouring red oxide dye mixed into the mud to simulate blood. Further, we'd settled on plastering the interior of the house with mud from a hill called *LaBahada,* a site we'd spotted on the way to Santa Fe, accessible from the highway. This earth was deep red, terracotta rich. We'd have to bring it home bucket by bucket. Then we found another streak of mud luck, a hill which was nearly purple. We'd used that dirt as well for interior plastering.

Our little *contretemps* over window heights, door frames and just about everything took time from our building. One day as we argued over four inches higher or lower for the windows, I remember thinking I might explode with details of house building. We waited until the kids were napping for our real doozies, knowing fighting upset them. This day they were back at home with the sitter.

The weight of this project was getting heavier. If anything went wrong, it was entirely our fault. No one to blame but ourselves. And in that frustrated state I decided it was time for action. Lee went back to troweling and I walked over to the wheelbarrow of mortar, oozy and ready to spread. I took off my work gloves and cupped as much as I could, walked over to Lee and thwacked a big load at his back. He turned in astonishment. Jose and Librano stopped working. Lee went over to the mud pit and scooped up an even larger handful and let me have it. The war was on.

"Ayudame, Librano!" I said. "Help me." For the next hour it was cowboys and Indians as Lee and Librano and I darted around the shell of our house throwing mud at one another. Librano got so tickled he would have to stop and slap his leg, he went back at giving Lee what for. Jose continued his dignified trolling, looking down sadly at the so-called adults performing what I thought was necessary "mud therapy." If I ever gave advice to couples who were building their own adobe I always whispered to the woman, "Start a mud fight. It's as good as sex."

Early on in the project we'd determined that we wanted our electricity and phone wires in trenches underground. When the trenches were dug for electricity, the phone company had agreed to lay down their lines\at the same time But the phone company never showed up. Every day I'd have to go to a booth right off the highway, asking them when they were coming. After two continual weeks the trenches had to be closed. That was the law. And what would the phone company do? They'd come back later and retrench to the tune of four thousand dollars. I was beginning to get a glimmer of how things worked in New Mexico. So we would have no phone. Out there on the mesa, with two small children and no telephone.

New Mexico is the perfect place to take up meditation, because everything in the world of commerce and bureaucracy makes a person like us want to tear his/her hair out. I tried to use friendly persuasion to get the phone company to comply and retrench, calling frequently to explain how difficult life would be with two babies, out on a mesa and no telephone. The standard reply went, "Well I don't know Mrs. Johnson."

And so I began my attack. My plan was a bit like the Civil War, an event supposedly lasting only a few months.

At first I tried calling the phone company from the Thunderbird. I chose this spot because I would at least be entertained by the writing on the wall next to the pay phone. Some of the sayings seemed to come from cowboy lore: "The only animal who sleeps with his eyes closed is dead." As I waited on the line I read further: "Cortez eats clay." The last bit of wisdom got into the trenches: "Mario fucks his goats. Don't eat his cheese."

At first I was given the same person in the personnel department, let's call him Mr. Ortega. I tried to appeal to his paternal side.

"Mr. Ortega, do you know what it's like to have children get sick in the night and not be able to contact a doctor?"

"Oh, si." I could hear him having a soft conversation with one of his pals at the phone company, the phone probably buried under his arm as I rattled on. So the next day I called and asked to speak to a woman, any woman.

"Mrs. Rodriquez, let me tell you what happened last night. Our son got hold of a bottle of cough medicine and drank the whole thing down in practically one swig."

I could hear her emery board scratching back and forth.

"Do you know what that means?"

"Huh?'

"Do you know what it means to have an emergency situation without a phone, your child's life at risk?"

"Not really."

"Well, I'll tell you then. First we had to rush to the nearest phone about four miles away right on the edge of the freeway. You know what trucks sound like." Then I made some whooshing sounds for the effect. She was silent.

"Okay, so here I am waiting for the doctor to call back on the freeway, a child nearly passed out, us forty-five minutes from the hospital. I was nearly crazy."

"Si."

At least we agreed on one thing. I continued. "So, then finally the doctor does call back but the clock is ticking away. He says to get some medication called Ipecac, ever hear of that?"

"Is that the stuff when you get the diarrhea?"

"No, Mrs. Rodriquez, this is to make your child puke."

"I think that my sister had that happen."

"Then you know what happens when you give that to a child."

"Not really."

"Okay, imagine projectile vomiting."

"What's that?"

"It means a child vomits so hard it flies out of him like he was being... " I searched for the right word, "exorcised."

"Your kid was exorcised? You got a devil in your house?"

"No, Mrs. Rodriguez, stay with me, please."

"Okay, but I got a break coming up. We get a break every hour."

"So, I forged on, "my poor son vomits so hard he is crying. Like it splattered all over the walls like a crime scene, you know when someone gets crazy and for no reason walks into a house or sometimes it's an office, any office, maybe with a gripe, you know for being ignored, and sometimes it might be an innocent place like the town hall or a school, sometimes places like telephone companies."

"Hold on," she said.

I waited. I heard a more official voice say, "This is customer service, can I help you?"

Day after day we ping ponged with the same call and response. But

I was tireless. I had only one weapon, my Scheherazade ability to keep telling them horror stories of my life without a phone. I talked about the night I nearly sliced my finger off making jewelry on a wheel. I told them about how our dog (fictional at that point) got into a fight with Leroy the mastiff from hell and how my husband nearly lost his hand to Leroy, I told them about the time banditos broke into our home and I couldn't call the police...

As I continued my tales I was interrupted by a male voice.
"Mrs. Johnson, we're going to put your phone. in.
"What?"
"How much?" I asked.
"We're doing it for free."
I looked out at the mesas, imagined Virga floating towards me reminding me the Land of Enchantment was also the land of *Milagros*.
We poured the four inches of mud in the zome living room.

I set up barriers so no one would wander in there while the floors were drying. Even though it was September, there was enough heat to dry the floors properly. Lee's university classes had started and so we weren't able to work every day, mostly weekends. We enrolled both children in the nearby Montessori school twice a week. As Lilah had the verbal skills of a three plus child, there was no problem enrolling her in the same group as Mogran. Suddenly I had the odd sense of time on my hands. It seemed like we'd grown time over the year. Jose and Librano took a short break and returned to their families in Mexico. Life seemed to be returning to normal, whatever that was.

Tenure for Lee was as far away as his fortieth birthday. Since this was his first foray into the university atmosphere, he had no idea what notes were being scribbled onto his "permanent record," the one which would determine whether or not he would keep his job. As we discovered later, it is possible to publish and to perish.

But the university calendar gave us holidays at beautiful times of the year. At fall break we traveled to Juarez to buy tiles. This was our first vacation away from the children. I'd found a sitter from the village who seemed more than competent. Janet always wore sensible clothing, no tattoos, she was demure and even though we were only to be gone two days, I made her memorize the number of our doctor, friends who lived nearby, family, etc. After all, what could happen in two days? Suddenly we realized we were actually getting there, we were going to break the ribbon over the finish line. The idea of buying brand new Mexican tiles sparked off our zeal to go to Juraz where all things Mexican were less then half price.

At dinner that night in Juarez we had a margarita. Then we had a second. My head was spinning, we were laughing, shrugging off all thoughts of what lay ahead, only toasting how much we'd gotten done. I had a surge of self-confidence, pride in our ability to slog through this unbelievable project.

After all the toasting, I had a thought. "You know what's odd?"

"What?" Lee was drawing something on the tablecloth with a swizzlestick. "My parents have never said a single word about our project, nothing.

"This is new?" Lee asked. We really had a laugh over that one.

My birthday was coming up. The only clue I got that my parents at least knew we were forging ahead with our house building showed up on my birthday. Inside a box was a new pair of work gloves. Happy Birthday, was written on the back of an old Christmas card. Actually, it was a wonderful and timely gift.

We were still renting a house in Corrales; but imagining the moving date on the calendar, we were ready to get into our house even though it wasn't complete. I'd spent hours in the zome living room filling in the tiny fissures and cracks in the mud floor, now dry enough to walk on. All of the floor in the zome had to be poured in one day, four inches thick of the sludge, so it looked uniform. Next it had to be leveled and left alone to dry.

I didn't know of anyone who was as intimate with their house as we were. Here I was, practically kissing the earthen floor, running my fingers over the cracked map, feeling the fissures and the valleys. I'd tried using a teaspoon to pour the mud slip into the cracks, but the spoon was not the right tool for the job. I had to go into our wedding silver and find a demitasse spoon. At last, a use for these refined eating utensils we got as wedding presents. I laughed as I thought of my mother stumbling into this scene, walking through our crude, unfinished house, bumping into the likes of Jerry in his leather dope-stuffed apron, or Jose and Librano taking a lunch break, playing with the kids or listening to the wrestling matches. Although only separated by four states, my New Orleans family was now continents away.

I watched the mud seep into the crack; I had to wait when an bubble caused resistance. This was a zen task, although I didn't know much about zen at that time. Looking at the design on the tiny silver spoon I was difference in my relationship to my former home and where I was now. I stopped and lay my cheek next to the drying floor, seeing all the fissures, touching the earth so intimately I would have blushed had anyone walked in. How many people can have this kind of close physical contact with their home? I felt as if I were having an affair with the earth. I was.

Miracles seemed to be part of the gross national product of New Mexico. One day I opened the paper to see a doleful woman holding up a tortilla. In its center was, by her calculations, the image of the Madonna. Pretty soon crowds came to see this milagro. Beneath it, a substantial altar with flowers, candles and letters.

My personal miracle was taking a day off from building as spending the night at La Fonda hotel in Santa Fe. The idea of an uninterrupted bath, a soak, was almost unbelievable. Could we afford this? Could we not? We wisely chose the path of pampering... we were weary, worn builders. Just one night. One full day. A dinner out. Silence.

While the South Valley claimed its miracle, there were every day *milagros* in Santa Fe as we discovered when we went to the large Basicila church on the *Zocalo,* Our Lady of Guadalupe. We happened to be there at the all-Mary runway show. A miniature statue of Mary was being dolled up for a special occasion by 'her ladies.' One woman took the time to talk about the honor of dressing *La Senora.* In a side chapel off the back, Mary's wardrobe shimmered and caught the light from the stained-glass window. From the look of things Barbie didn't have anything over Mary. And the small Spanish woman began to show us Mary's favorite robes flashing red satin with gold embroidery. "This is one of her favorites," she told us.

"How do you know she has a preference?" I said.

"My lady just won't wear certain dresses. She struggles against them. Believe me, if she don't want to wear it, she won't."

I liked the idea of Mary being so fashion conscious.

We found more miracles in Chimayo, a small town in the north east of Santa Fe. We entered a small church through an adobe court-yard. Two bells hung in the towers.

We discovered the small room called *el pocito*, the location for the pit filled with fine, silty dirt which, some say, has healing powers. I watched some pilgrims rub dirt all over their arms and legs, then scoop up some and put it in a Mayonnaise jar like leftover food from a restaurant.

On the wall in the interior of the church silver *milagros* of legs, arms, eyes, hearts and, for the gastricly distressed, an abdomen. Personal letters of thanks for the healing, all hand scribbled, dangled next to testimonials. A few crutches leaned against the altar, the spongy tops dirty and frayed. It was a sweet church built in the late 19th century, the interior reminding me of medieval churches in France, beautiful in its simplicity.

Before we left I decided to scrape up dirt and put it in a zip lock. Miracles seemed to be part of the gross national product of New Mexico.

Mark and Kay's home was hand built right next to the national forest; we could smell the green breath of the forest and hear the low whistle of wind in the trees. When I showed them my bag of dirt, they told us Mark's parents had just visited in the spring, taking home a similar bag to show their friends in the synagogue. A week after their return to New York, Mark's dad wrote a letter. "The healing dirt really works, wow. But now I don't know what to send back to hang on the wall."

"What was his ailment," I asked. "Hemorrhoids," Mark replied.

The real miracle in our lives was we'd *almost* moved into the house, but still had dirt floors throughout except for the poured mud floor in the Zome. I wish our *caliche* floors had some kind of sacred quality to them but I couldn't see evidence of that. And because of the altitude drop in the children's section, gratis to Jerry and his merry pranksters, the floors sloped dramatically down to their bedroom and ours. It was perfect for riding trucks and wagons to bed, much like the runaway truck ramp on freeways. What had run away in our lives was our budget.

One topic went unaddressed in the villages we visited in New Mexico. The subject was the *penitentes*. The word *morada* often arose in conjunction with this group. The first time I saw one called by name happened on a visit to a reconstructed village outside of Santa Fe called Los Ranchos de las Golandrinas. It was after Easter and the sky was robin's egg blue. The dust storms hadn't begun, and you could legitimately claim this spot on the planet was the land of enchantment. We were guided through a living history museum constructed in 1700, an adobe compound with Russian olives and the scent of water flowing nearby. The guide told us this place was the last stop of El Camino Royale. But one building in this place caught my attention in its starkness. When I asked what it was the guide said a *"morada, "* then moved us to the stables and the farm to see authentic cattle and hear bugling roosters.

No one in our village talked much about the present-day use of a *morada*. What I gathered was it was used on Good Friday to wash the body of the represented Jesus when he was taken off the cross. It is a secret society comprised of *hermanos,* brothers. A no girls-allowed club. And if I heard the rumors correctly, some person is elected to be Jesus. Like the Mayan ball games, if you win, you lose....your head. Being chosen to stand in for Christ is like being elected King of Carnival by your community's brotherhood. Except in New Orleans the King of Carnival has fun. His suffering is usually a gigantic hangover. Jesus just suffers. And apparently not just on Good Friday. During Holy Week he has to contemplate his soul, salvation, he has to walk around some similarity of the Garden of Gethsemane knowing someone is going to betray him. The hooded society of *Hermanos,* equally have a task to walk around suffering, actually wishing for pain. And this *faux* Jesus, chosen by the community, has to drag his cross up a hill, being whipped and physically abused. He's supposed to say things like "Whip me, flail me." His duty is to suffer and bleed. Even *ask* for the nails on the cross as the five wounds are inflicted. An elected Jesus is a subject of great pride for the family of this man. I heard different reports as to whether the brothers, *las hermanos,* were actually connected to the priest of their church. I heard officially the church would not be connected to this group. I just remember one stark fact. The day I visited the *morada* at the Rancho de las Golandrinas, the trough-like tub in the stripped-down room was dark with moisture. As if someone had recently taken a bath.

New Mexico in the fall was clean and clear, as if the entire state had been through a car wash. Down in the valley the cottonwoods were turning yellow, and a *piñon* crispness settled around us. I'd been listening to the wind since we had partially moved up to the house. Now rain was no longer a threat as we had windows and doors; in fact as it drummed on the Zome roof it often sounded like applause to me. The shadows outside became more delineated and everyone talked of the first snow. Up at the Thunderbird there were wagers for the right snow date.

Fall was another reason to celebrate: it was harvest season. According to Jerry the best dope came from a place called Fervent Valley. Jerry expounded so generously on the bouquet of the gifts from this commune, Lee talked me into a trip there. I was the designated driver long before such a term existed. But I wanted to arrive home intact.

The roads in New Mexico can be treacherous. They form long wavy ribbons across the landscape, then suddenly veer to the right and jog back for no good reason. After a heavy rain, cars easily hydroplane as if on ice. It is beside these odd departures white crosses and plastic flowers are often planted.

Looking back on the fall with its gracious light and sweet garden offerings, I also remember that the joyous feeling of expansion had a slight edge to it. That over-zealous celebration of plenty had a desperate underpinning called winter. Winter meant frozen ground, bitter wind, cabin fever. "Enjoy the warmth while you can," Jerry offered up our first season out on the mesa. There was just a soupçon of malice to his words.

Either stoned or straight, Fervent Valley was like finding a valley of paradise hidden behind clumps of trees. It had rained the day before so the roads were slick, the car kept sliding this way and that which the kids loved. Those kinds of roads give me a sickening feeling, reminding me of the time we were stranded in a commune in northern New Mexico during a blizzard. Even in the largest space God ever created, such situations caused claustrophobia in my innards.

Before we arrived we heard the drumming. Occasional yelps and claps brought us closer to a celebration of fall beyond the outrageous fol. With the clarity of the air, the brilliant blue sky, everything had a translucent aura: the yurt structure, smoke curling out, the clump of bamboo making a small groaning sound that reminded me of big knuckles rubbing together, the big muddy pond filled with naked hippies. This place was as exotic as Morocco, the air burning with dope, patchouli smelling smoke and the physicality of a new dimension. I saw a child who appeared to be about four walk up to his mother and began sucking on her teat. I turned to Lee. "Where are we, Borneo?"

Someone had constructed an altar of squash, pumpkins and everything that burst yellow and gold in the fall. Marigolds surrounded the vegetables and a great vase of sunflowers stood tall turning their faces to the diminishing sun. This was a vegetarian version of Mardi Gras.

All fall I watched the ghostly *Virga* sweeping across the mesas in our direction. It was easy to hallucinate up there without the benefit of drugs. Virga, like the Madonna, reached for us, the withholding gauzy mother, then holding back.

One day I stood next to Jerry who'd dropped by to see how the interior of our house was progressing. I could tell he was disgusted with our normal straight walls and viga ceilings. We were looking at the mesas when he said, *"Virga, she's such a teasing bitch,"* he said. We watched the gauze wafting in our direction for a while.

"Oral Roberts is coming to Albuquerque," he said out of nowhere.

"I don't go for those snake oil salesmen," I said.

"All kinds of religion tucked away in New Mexico.

"I saw the Mormons are opening something in Bernalillo," I said. "Yeah. Arf is going there. They watch her kids."

"Mom's morning out?"

"Sorta." He took a splif and lit it, pointed in my direction. "No, thanks. Makes me either paranoid or hungry."

"See, the way I see it, this place, the mesas, Ship Rock," he made a sweeping gesture with his hand, the smoke trailing behind it, "it's like that ride at the state fair. The Rotor."

"You mean the thing that spins around in circles and the bottom drops out and you stick to the sides.

"Dig it. See hidden up in the mesas there's Indians, shamans, hippies, aura people... they got sick of religion, so they spun out into the comers, hiding. Those are the sacred ones," he concluded.

"No doubt," I agreed. "No doubt."

I always envied the rituals and secrecy of the Catholic church, the religion that predominated New Orleans. But I grew up Presbyterian, steeped in guilt. Sometimes our minister would fly into such a rage at the sin around us (did he notice it was New Orleans?) it looked as if he might go aloft like a hot air balloon, screaming at us, particularly the teenage section of the audience.

So when I discovered the sacred com dances held at the nearby pueblo of Santa Ana, I was intrigued and knew this was a rare opportunity to see a ceremony in a culture also steeped in secrecy. I was furthering my thirst for a connection to the cosmos, a different sense of the sacred. I'd seen these Indians shopping in the Bernalillo mercantile in town, always laden with turquoise, feathers in their hair, long-braided women, men with shells hung around their necks. I wanted to see how sacred manifested in dance.

The com dances are held on August 4th beginning with a marriage ceremony in the morning honoring couples who'd married during the year. Friends had warned us the dances were long, lasting into the evening. But we were eager to attend an event as this pueblo was open to the public only a few days a year.

Oddly this Indian tradition began in a Catholic church dedicated to Saint Dominic. Bells rang, muskets fired and St. Dominic was lifted like a Jewish bride, carried through the village. Sharing this harvest dance with the world at large is a generous gift from the people of the pueblo and I remember standing in the stupefying sun while the entire village gathered to honor their saint's day and a day of prayers for rain and fructification. I was thirsty as cotton.

It was one of those days when the clouds banked and promised showers, but like *virga,* they only teased rain. Puffy doesn't describe the massed white cumulus whites floating in the sky. These clouds that mushroomed together seemed to have a purpose, the clumping of a secret society choosing who should get rain, who should not. These clouds, like the dancers below, carried an ancient and powerful spirit. The Eskimos have many names for snow. People of the desert have just as many for corn: masa, tablita. Corn is a separate food group in the Southwest.

I recognized familiar faces from the university that day, women dressed in long cotton skirts and enormous hats carrying bottles of water. All cameras had to be stowed according to the rules of the pueblos. There was an academic/anthropological sameness in those faces I knew from University socials, contrapuntal to the hippies in cut-off jeans, women showing way too much skin for this sacred event, babies thrown over their backs in imitation of the Indian papoose. The sun caught the nose rings of the young man, the belly button hoop in a woman I recognized from the Thunderbird named Rosie.

When the men first emerged from the *kiva* it was like seeing a horror film: their bodies were slaked in mud, their faces stark white, eyes ringed in black, com husks rustling around their heads; rabbit-skins representing the spirits of the dead, dangled from their waists. Morgan's eyes widened as the men approached our spot. He climbed into my lap.

The chanting began, the drumming of the tom-toms, the rattling of gourds, the sound of shells hitting shells that were tied to the ankles of the dancers. The sun tormented us as we sat on an itchy green army blanket watching the monotonous ceremony, both hypnotic and boring. I began to suspect that the road to salvation was paved with ennui. After two hours our water bottle was moving towards empty. I kept glancing at the sky, breathing in the yellow dust, waiting for the god to appear. Our children were restless, pulling at their hats, digging in the dirt with spoons we'd brought for our picnic lunch. But the children from that pueblo were as disciplined as the soldiers in front of Buckingham Palace. And those children were all wearing wool.

I didn't know the history of the pantomime I was watching but felt it was somehow historical, as if the Indians were protecting their pueblo from advancing enemies. The game we played as children flashed across my mind... Cowboys and Indians. I guessed the wild gesticulations and whoops meant either a war dance or something like Mardi Gras, the feast before the famine.

I'd seen something like this carrying of the saint through the streets of Italy once. It was a "saint race," a *los santos* marathon. It was pouring rain that day in Italy and the crowd kept telling us *"piu piove, pui festa,"* the more it rains, the better the festival. The favored saints were carried on a platform on the shoulders of burly men displaying their rippling arms as they ran up the side of a mountain. Inside gilded cages the seated saints shook back and forth creating a wobbly look reminding me of the back of a Mardi Gras float.

The crowds were Mardi Gras raucous chasing the procession up the hill, screaming and shouting as if it were the last lap of the *palio*.

This pueblo procession, on the other hand, was silent and respectful except for the presence of a man who was like the clown in the Shrine Circus. He leapt and pranced, making pantomime-like gestures meant to entertain the crowd. The entire village participated that day clear down to the sweating toddlers. In those long hours the cadence was foot-to-earth heavy. Women went barefoot to enhance their connection to mother earth who might help with the production of not just corn, but babies.

The deep rich calls from the dancing villagers shook the air, combined with heavy chanting, tom-tom beating and the sound of small bells and shells were overwhelming. It would not have surprised me if the earth had opened up and taken us into the deep kiva of secret rituals. Prancing, spinning and stamping. But above all the other sounds that day, the most enduring for me was the rustling of the corn husks worn by the men. Trance dancing erased all time. It was all dip, sway, sun, heat, dust, shells, rattles, husks.

I imagined the others there were like me, thirsting for something our culture didn't give us freely, something we had to beg for. I was beginning to think all ideas of the sacrosanct were like mirages, waving heat images like spirits throwing down the keys to the kingdom and waiting to see if we'd reach out. Deep voices kept calling out for rain for their crops piercing the air like javelins. And just at this moment of doubt, the heavens opened up. It poured. The village kept dancing, not breaking cadence, hardly noticing its prayers had been answered.

PART III

By Thanksgiving we were running out of time. It was a cold year, the temperatures dropping below freezing, snow falling on the Sandias. When mortar begins to freeze, it is useless to build. The elements remind you of the seasons: when to quit and hunker down. But we decided to push on anyway.

Jose and Librano were celebrating Thanksgiving with their adopted American families, though I doubt they fully understood the entire pilgrim/Indian thing. Or perhaps they understood the holiday more than we appreciated. We begged them to work just a half day on Thanksgiving so they could still enjoy their meal, and we had a sense of moving forward. It was a bitter day with wind-swept clouds, nothing to stop the winds out there on the mesa, either, plains making the junipers whistle in a way that reminded me of old radio shows.

On the way to Librano's we drove through back streets of Bernalillo. Signs of Christmas were already up, a neon flashing sign of the Madonna and child in a small adobe home, white flocked trees with blue lights in picture windows.

"I always find these flashy Mexican trappings endearing rather than tacky," I said.

We passed a cardboard creche, the wind had toppled one of the wise men. It looked as if they were about to give a gift to the baby Jesus, but tripped over something and fell at his feet. Something about this clumsy frozen moment made me sad. I turned to Lee.

"Why do we have to work on Thanksgiving Day? This is insane."

"We have to get the doorway up or all the mortar will freeze, you know that."

"You're so driven. We could wait until tomorrow, couldn't we?"

"Snowstorm coming." He pointed to the mountains.

We've been working in intermittent snow for weeks. I need a break."

"Why didn't you stay home, then?"

"And be the wimp who didn't show up in the blizzard?" "I didn't say that.

"You implied it."

"When?"

"This morning when I said I wish we could just fix a turkey like the rest of America." I turned sideways. "Besides it isn't right to drag these guys out on Thanksgiving Day."

"You think Thanksgiving has a significance for two exicans?"

"Sure. They have families here."

"Do you want me to turn around and take you home?"

!"We have to stop," I said. "One more row," Lee said. "Only one."

If building in the heat was miserable, building in the freezing winter was much worse. And of course, as we had been warned, it was a fruitless endeavor. By the time we cleaned our site it was snowing. The wind was biting. The adobes were falling like trees in a forest. When the first one hit the earth it made a solid thunking sound. The cold and the wind had joined hands and done their best to undo our day's work. Suddenly the entire doorway structure fell like a building being detonated.

We drove home in silence. "I told you so. Our season of building is over. Thank God. It will be Spring before the weather will be warm enough to continue."

Lee gritted his teeth as we wrapped sheets of plastic around our walls, watching it flap in a ghostly way. I didn't want to cry mostly because my tears might have frozen like Christmas ornaments on my face.

It snowed for Christmas, a New Orleanian's dream. The night we bundled up to celebrate Christmas, the air was pungent with *pinon,* the whole section called "Old Town," the oldest section of Albuquerque, was lit by soft *luminarias.* We walked through pushing Lilah in her baby buggy wrapped in blankets against the freezing cold. I'd found an old time perambulator at good will, the kind I remembered on the street where Christopher Robin lived in London. It had a plastic cover that snapped on three sides as well as a bonnet, giving Lilah the best protection possible. I was not used to the bitterness of New Mexico's winter. Wind sliced through us as we walked through the streets stopping to hear carolers. Someone had made a peace symbol in their yard with their luminaries, it looked magical in the snow. I wondered if Morgan would remember our Christmas night when he grew older. I tried hard to produce moments for them that might flicker later in their lives. The smell of snow and pinon, the glow of the lights in their small white bags.

Then it got even colder. Trees were so scarce in New Mexico we constructed a Christmas tree by stacking graduated tumble weeds, then wrapped what we could without snaring ourselves, with tiny white lights. I was determined to use our creativity to make a beautiful tree. The lights looked beautiful as they peeked through the thorns. As long as none of us touched the tree, it held an aura of magic.

When we lived in our home and became part of the rituals of the village we'd join in the *posada,* the procession that wove through the small streets of our village. It was a sweet memory as the donkey ridden by Mary, led by Joseph stopped at predetermined homes and the outcasts asked for room in the inn. Inside these candle lit homes a chorus of response sang in Spanish. Basically they were saying *get out of town,* but softly. The children were with us as we followed the trail of villagers in this Christmas sacrament.

When the donkey stopped at the last adobe home for yet one more choral rejection, it relieved itself on the dirt street. The kids, along with their friends, began to giggle. Mary, a.k.a. Starla, turned in her saddle to give them a frown. Lilah instantly recognized her. "That's not Mary, that's Starla." And then the war was on. "She picks her nose," said Dominic. "She farts all the time," said another. By the time we arrived at the gym, the doors that finally opened for them, the kids were unstoppable with their comments and laughing.

People were visiting us in droves by this time, often friends of friends showing up unexpectedly, a bottle of wine, a big smile. As it was winter, our building had slowed down, nearly halted. We were still in our small rented house in Corrales.

It got even colder. Trees were so scarce in New Mexico we constructed a Christmas tree by stacking graduated tumble weeds, then wrapped what we could without snaring ourselves, with tiny white lights. I was determined to use our creativity to make a beautiful tree.

The lights looked beautiful as they peeked through the thorns. As long as none ofus touched the tree, it held an aura of magic.

When we lived in our home and became part of the rituals of the village we'd join in the *posada,* the procession that wove through the small streets of our village. It was a sweet memory as the donkey ridden by Mary, led by Joseph stopped at predetermined homes and the outcasts asked for room in the inn. Inside, these candle lit homes a chorus of response sang in Spanish. Basically they were saying *get out of town,* but softly and in key. The children were with us as we followed the trail of villagers in this Christmas sacrament. When the donkey stopped at the last adobe home} it relieved itself on the dirt street. The kids, along with their friends, began to giggle. Mary, a.k.a. Starla, turned in her saddle to give them a frown. Lilah instantly recognized her. "That's not Mary, that's Starla." And then the war was on. "She picks her nose," said Dominic. "She farts all the time," said another. By the time we arrived at the gym, the doors that finally opened for the faux holy family, the kids were unstoppable with their comments and laughing. Lilah grew into the one who noticed the emperor wore no clothes, this became her personal stamp, the finger pointer.

One particularly cold night some strangers showed up, friends of old friends from New Orleans who had given our names to them at a party. Party? New Orleans? Where else? I could imagine them all gathered around the table laden with oyster patties, daube glace, party sandwiches, the bourbon flowing freely.

Generally we had a one-night rule for folks who fell into that third party friend category, but the temperature plummeted. By midnight it was zero. The next day a blizzard, a white out. The third day, it was close to twenty-five below zero. No one could get their car started. Phones didn't work. Walking outside was treacherous and no emergency vehicle could get anywhere on the icy roads, even the freeway. We were stuck with Jan and Dennis. We were running out of butane. Food. Firewood. Patience. All pipes had frozen, no running water meant latrine living in the bathroom. After the second record-breaking night we'd run out of food entirely and were left with marshmallows and banana liquer. And our guests. These were the Southwest versions of *The Man Who Came To Dinner.* By three a.m. on the third night, we started burning chairs. They were the Mexican-type with straw seats that flared when thrown in the fireplace, giving us a momentary thrill and not much heat. Dennis spoke.

"We've never done this before."

Done what?" Lee asked wrapping the children in coats. "Crashed on strangers."

"You're friends with Walter and Sandra," I said, trying not to think of how we'd survive if they didn't leave. Thoughts of the Donner party kept pushing into my brain.

"Well"

"Well, what?" Lee asked.

"We don't really know them."

"You mean you don't know them well?"

"No. We don't know them at all. We just heard them talking about friends in New Mexico. They jotted down your names." He pulled out a scrap of paper with our phone number.

Across the fire threshold Lee and I exchanged looks. "As soon as you can get your car going," Lee said. "You are out of here."

At first thaw, we pushed them onto a road. As soon as we could make phone calls we called Walter and Sandra. Collect.

During our building era we found many treasures at the Bernalillo dump. Used rebar, old bricks, scratched up doors, cabinets that could be painted. At Christmas it seemed like a good time to give back to the dump that which it had given to us. After all the opening of presents we packed up the presents we knew we would never use, such things as a popcorn popper, a wine opener that didn't work, socks that didn't fit any of us, scented candles that smelled like toilet bowl cleaners and a hand-knitted scarf that must have come from a church rummage sale.

"Who wants to pretend to be Santa?" I said.

Each unusable gift was carefully re-wrapped. "God Rest Ye Merry Gentlemen," we sang on the way to the dump.

We had the foresight to bring an old blue cloth we'd used as cover for the children's geodesic dome in the summer, turning the metal structure into an igloo, a fort, a hidey hole for the kids. When we got to the dump we were the only people about. We began constructing our altar using the blue cloth as a drape. On top, the candles were set in a row, then the popcorn popper, then all the other things we would never use. It wasn't long before the scavengers appeared. And so we hid behind a mound of smoking garbage in a scene that might have come from a Dickens novel. Crouched down Morgan began to giggle. I put my finger to my mouth and lured both children into this conspiracy.

It took the family about twenty minutes to kick through the broken scooters, the chairs with two legs, the broken tea pot. They spotted our altar.

"Ah, Chihuahua!" the mother shouted and began running towards our shrine. The children ripped into the presents, excited by the possibility of a real Santa Claus out there. The mother sniffed the noxious candle and rolled her eyes heavenwards. The father wrapped the gray and red scarf around his neck looking like a lost Christmas caroler. We all stayed down, Lee pointing to his lips again. The kids didn't make a sound that might ruin the solemnity of this moment.

Bond beams and Spring are reasons for hope. You are nearly there. Once the winds died down, the tamarisk trees fluffed pink. Even the cactus showed up, though not like magnolias. Spring in the desert is all about surprise. Tiny pin cushions spring into large crimson blossoms. Purple, magenta, orange and red flowers appear like bright Easter eggs. We wanted to thank each and every one. One day Lilah leaned over in a stance like her great grandmother, hand on hip, finger pointing to the ground. "Where have you been?" She said. "We've been waiting for you."

Bond beams tie all the adobes together; they are the glue and it doesn't matter how strong the adobe walls are, without this mighty collar the whole place could crumble. Rebar is pounded into the adobe bricks before the cement in the bond beam is poured; they stick up around the perimeter of the house like pilings in lakes.

Zeke always told us these facts with a slight grin on his face, mentioning the threat of occasional earthquakes. "One good earthquake and ka blooey." To illustrate this he picked up a crumbling adobe from the graveyard of not-quite-right bricks and pulverized it in his hand. Then he broke into his old-time-movie laugh.

Wooden forms have to be made to pour the concrete in that makes up the levee fortress called the bond beam. Inside those forms, rebar helps secure the structure.

Thank God Jose and Librano reminded us of the wooden lintels that needed to be laid over the windows and doors. We had to scamper the hills and mesas to find wood that was strong, but had an antique and ravaged appearance. Nothing was going to look new.

We built battered walls on the North side of our house where they weren't really needed. We wanted the Ranchos de Taos Pueblo effect. And we'd decided to give the main entry of our home an extra exotic effect, like pylon gates doorways to the Temple of Thebes at Tizin. We had to begin again with the failed building that Thanksgiving Day.

Like us, Jose and Librano were energized by the change in season. We'd come to depend on their building intelligence as well as their extra set of eyes now that the children were up on the land more frequently. To keep the kids entertained, we splurged on two big wheels they could ride up and down our traffic-free road. Lilah was highly competitive with her big brother. They raced along the bumpy dirt track, the noise of the plastic wheels sounding more impressive by the scattering pebbles and flying dirt. Their big wheels had the same amplification of bicycles with playing cards affixed to the tires. We figured as long as they were slathered with suntan lotion, hydrated and fed they'd be okay. But then the road became silent in ways that make a parent vigilant. I looked up in time to see Lilah defying the laws of gravity, flying over the side towards the arroyo below. All four of us were set into gear scrambling down the crumbly mesa sideways hoping to find her in one piece. She was gathering her dignity when we got to her, not even crying, but visibly shaken. Looking up I caught Morgan peering over the side. It didn't take a rocket scientist to recreate this scene, Morgan daring her to fly. Lilah, our lion daughter, taking on the challenge. We would all have to grow a few more eyes. It didn't help that Jerry said we should let her "fly like Johnathan Livingston Seagull."

I snapped back with "A child doesn't really have a higher purpose like that bird was supposed to have."

It was now time to make a decision about plumbing and wiring.

Everybody in our community bartered. But we couldn't find something as a bartering tool as we didn't have the strength to help build another house while working on our own. I'd watched a family score the interior walls of their adobes readying it for wires and plumbing pipes.

We hesitated to ask about who might do this, knowing Zeke would have someone, but likely someone who'd lifted the pipes from another construction site. I had visions of someone driving up to our completed home and demanding their pipes back, then hosing down the walls, grabbing their pipes and leaving us with gaping portals.

Normally, a bid is put out for plumbers and electricians, but since nothing we did in this house project was normal, we eschewed the "Square Dude from Illinois" path, (Jerry's continual reference to our neighbor with the Quaid fence). Jerry's idea of a septic tank was two sticks of dynamite at sunset.

We listened hard over Jerry Jeff Walker's voice at the Thunderbird Bar trying to garner some information about a reliable plumber. As it happened, a family was building a house nearby. They were an offshoot from Jerry's "free form," had about three and a half kids and a scattered number of pets. I finally figured out that we had one thing we could barter in the present and in the future. I could cook big meals for their family and in the future they could bathe at our house. It seemed like a fair trade. After all, the pipes and whatnot were glued together and the job of scraping out the adobe walls was something we could do ourselves. We used gravity as our guide to pull waste into the sewage field and septic tank. (Jerry's idea) The pipes needed to be vented, that was simple enough. And the drainage field needed perforated pipe in case the system got overloaded. A percolation test for the soil seemed silly to us, one of those mandates made up in Los Alamos between bomb testings. And so we made a handshake deal with Bob and his runny-nosed tribe. His plumbing, our food and future facilities. At the time most of the folks around us were loaded, as in dope or acid or even locoweed. Bob and his family were no exception. They had absolutely no control of their children and I often saw his wife, nicknamed Arf because when she laughed she sounded like a dog, looking about as if she were counting heads but forgetting how many children they'd begotten. These kids were sick all the time. I could barely stand looking at the noses and insisted they wipe faces before they ate one of the many meals I prepared for them. The problem with this bartering system was figuring out when the balance sheet was right. How many meals equaled a day of scoring walls? I realized I'd made a deal I now wished to break. And the worst was yet to come: the baths.

During the time of plumbing excavation and finished bathrooms the family had evolved from LSD to LDS. The Mormons had taken them under their wing. Once we had functioning bathrooms we were dealing with lectures about the angel Moroni. I'd never heard of such stuff as the golden tablets reportedly found by Joseph Smith. I didn't see what was wrong with caffeine or wine and I sure didn't like the way the newly converted were laying bible and verse on me and I suspected Arf was passing some spun home theology in the children's direction. I was respectful when we broke bread together while we all bowed our heads and said a blessing. That seemed reasonable to me.

They'd found a new way to rapture and began producing offspring in an alarming fashion. I couldn't keep track of the children when they came calling.

It was true the church had mandated a cleanup over there. And Arf began wearing clothes reminiscent of Conestoga wagon days: all long skirts, modest blouses and covered head. At the end of our project, bathrooms finished, they began to pile in for their Saturday night baths. I was still figuring out the cost of heating water for that many folks as well as cooking one large meal. When they arrived, they had forgotten essentials like soap, shampoo, wash cloths. I insisted they bring their own towels. They did remember a rubber ducky now and then. But when they left, the bathroom was like the locker room at the Y after swim class for toddlers. Bits of Pampers clung to our brick floor and the ring around the tub rivaled the rings around Saturn. Things came to a rather unpleasant end when I blew up after the last of the tribe had their Saturday ablutions.

"Not once," I said, "NOT ONE SINGLE TIME have you ever cleaned the tub when you took a bath."

Arf had managed a new expression of guilt and sorrow that reflected her new leanings. But she fell into silence rather than take any responsibility for their sloppy habits. Bob led a few of the kids out the front door as Arf talked about the bible.

"We're even. We are completely even," I said. She left with a hang-dog look, a child in hand. I had the horrible feeling she might be praying for me.

One lingering after affect made me consider where we were vis a vis our children's religious upbringing. Lee thoroughly despised organized religion and there didn't seem to be many alternatives between the Catholic church, the Presbyterians and the aura balancers. So we let that part of their lives slide. Some of my unhappiest memories as a child were connected to the vacation Bible school. I didn't want to repeat that mistake. One day as I was adding up the week's expenditures on flapping yellow receipts I heard the kids speaking in low tones. They were not on their Big Wheels or under their make-shift Indian bedspread tent. I walked around trying to follow the thread of their voices and stopped beside a large juniper. Under it the two of them had made a kind of altar with a candle and some rocks. They were on their knees. I held my breath and wondered what they might be thirsting for.

It's all about water and water rights in the Southwest and especially in our village.

Hispanic families tried to keep the dormant irrigation ditches flowing for fear of losing them. Water rights could be bought, sold and transferred. There was tremendous fraud in this system. New developments on the mesa and things like golf courses had brought serious changes in the land and raised much ire with the old timers as well as those who were recently converted New Mexicans. The ditches that carried life to the fields and homes are as old as three hundred years, much like the old Roman aqueducts. Of course within the communities there is lots of bribery, particularly with the person in charge of the water rights, the *mayordomo,* also known as the ditch boss.

Spring in our village was celebrated each year with an event called "Ditch Day." Most of the small houses in the village had large tracts of land for gardens irrigated by the long ditches that lay side by side in the rich earth. All winter the ditches accumulated garbage: tumbleweed, plastic bottles and beer cans. Come spring the entire village participated in this cleansing except for people, like our friends, who had been shunned from the event and from getting access to water because they abused the system. Our friends made the mistake of washing their car. In our gossipy village if someone transgressed like that, they could bank on being turned in, turned away. It didn't help that the perpetrators were a hippy poet and his wife known to wear a ballerina outfit everywhere even though she didn't dance. Their children were dressed imaginatively, but normally went unwashed. The village kids reminded me of old film clips from our gang, scrappy kids who ran around the streets unsupervised, ending up at Lizzie's grocery where they were sure to get free candy.

On Ditch Day as everyone hoed, dug, pitched and burned, our outcast friends watched from their side of the fence.

The ditch boss cracked the whip at dawn and nobody quit until the water ran unencumbered, sluicing into fields as alfalfa and chile began to make their bright green appearance. We all learned about water preservation when we lived in New Mexico, to brush our teeth, spit out the toothpaste, then drink from a cup rather than allow precious water to run down the drain. As Jerry had told us when we first arrived on our property, "About seven inches of water a year is about all we get." We were used to that amount falling in one day in New Orleans. We had to learn about conservation, sometimes showering with a bucket in the shower so we could then use the overflow to irrigate our plants. That meant no caustic soap in the tub. Everything affected everything.

Even though we didn't live in the village, we felt connected to community there and tried to be useful on "Ditch Day" by picking up trash or raking the banks. This gave us a false sense of righteousness we easily translated into an evening at the Thunderbird Bar where everyone had a story about their trials and tribulations, the crap they had to haul, the bragging rights about who had the most garbage, the sunburned arms, the sweaty shirts a badge of honor no one would think of changing before showing up for the annual party.

It was as raucous as a cage of parrots that night, but there was a particular buzz going around. Everyone was yammering about a guy named John. Finally our friend Jensen gave us the full scoop.

"Like you know how it is the night before "Ditch Day," he said swilling the beer we'd just paid for. "Everybody gets wound up, the ditch boss comes in and tells everybody to settle down. More or less like the football coach telling the team no sex before the game." He nodded towards Charlie Mendosa, this year's boss. "Of course once he was out of the door, the party got way loud." Jensen glad-handed a friend, then returned to the story.

"So last night Luke and Jason were having an acid off."

"Want to explain that?" I asked.

"You know, one hit for me, one hit for you. More or less dope till you drop. They don't have gardens, so they didn't give a shit about being out in the sun today or doing a lick of work. They're both pretty laid back."

I glanced around for the vestiges of these two guys who normally could be found in the comers, then pulled up to the bar officially when the sun went down, more or less like reptiles.

"A few guys joined in, it was getting macho and weird like watching a psychedelic chess match. People with serious irrigation needs cut out early, scared the ditch boss might find out they'd broken curfew. The bar was pretty drained by midnight. That's how come nobody much noticed what Luke had done." He paused and sucked down the foam left in his glass.

"I'll get the next one," Lee said signaling the bar tender. We both get anxious if a good story is interrupted. Clearly, if we wanted the whole story we'd have to buy him off. Once the foam hit the top level he said, "Luke had shoved a hunting knife clear into his forehead. I don't mean a little ways, that sucker was in there."

"God almighty," Lee said.

"Yeah. And dig this, he was still alive. So the entire stoned crew got him to his feet and decided they'd better not pull the thing out. Better to get to B.C.M.C. pronto."

"What a weird night," I said imagining one of those trick knife gizmos people wear to costume parties, making it look as though there's a dagger plunged into their brains.

"It gets better," Jensen said. "About halfway down to Bernalillo, Hank's truck broke down. And these guys aren't mechanics plus they've put away about six tabs each. So they're stumbling all over the highway. Hank gets the idea they'd better hitch into town. Luke's in some weird state with the knife still pointing North, the acid turning his brain around like a ball in the lotto."

"Did anyone pick them up?" I said wondering how it would be to come across this crew, thumbs out, knife in.

"Yeah, finally, some poor dude heading for town stopped, he

thought the knife thing was a joke, until Luke got into his car. Then the guy freaked. He got them all to the emergency room, but Jeez, what a scene in there. Saturday night in the ER in Albuquerque is already a circus. The guy on duty had to call a brain surgeon in."

"Did he live?"

"Oh, yeah. But man, he gave himself a lobotomy. The doc said if he tried, he could not have stuck that blade in him and not killed him. He's gonna have quite a ride for the rest of his life."

"What about the others? They must have freaked out," Lee said.

"I saw Hank today. He's thinking about getting a bumper sticker made with that punch line, "I'd rather have a bottle in front of me then a frontal lobotomy."

"You mean as some weird object message?"

"No, man. The idea is to sell the stickers to raise funds for Luke. After all he's going to be a vegetable all his life. But it was a *milagro* he lived."

The village was made more interesting by the preponderance of poets who lived there. Most notably, Robert Creeley. Creeley, as everyone called him, was a soft spoken person with few words aloud. I figured he saved the good stuff for the page. But at one party he was uncommonly vociferous. I leaned against an adobe wall as he rattled on about the person who was renting his house in the village, a wench from New Orleans named Veronica. I knew her, she had the voice of a Brooklyn crow and was given to rages. She refused to let him into his property and didn't pay the rent. Unfortunately, I learned for the first time, the law is on the side of the tenant. She'd driven poor Creeley to distraction. He said he couldn't think straight. She stood in front of his door and screamed invectives at him, made his life miserable from dawn til dusk. From everything he said, I imagined she'd more or less obliterated his muse. And because of her he decided to leave the village. I sat on an adobe wall talking to Lee in undertones.

"Did you hear what 'you know who' did to Creeley?"

"Bitch. She has some weird tendencies. That temper. A real rage-a-holic." "Someone told me she and her husband had a terrific fight which resulted with him leaving on his motorcycle in a huff. You can guess what happened."

I played with the foil around the top of my beer bottle. "Let's never let a fight get us that crazy. Please." I remembered the words we often heard, as indelible now as the faces on Mount Rushmore: "You may build the house, but you won't stay married."

The migration of hippies and far out folks included a great dose of what we now call "healers." I'd noticed the dynamics of a commune when we'd spent time during a blizzard and got snowed in. There was always a power grab, even though no one wanted to own this hierarchy, "too much like the military-industrial-complex," but it was there.

Before we moved into our Placitas home, still living in Corrales, a group was springing up in the North Valley that professed to "change your life." Just out of curiosity, we attended one of the miracle meetings. There, in front of us stood what might be described as the class nerd. He already had a following, but not me. This guy was an off-shoot from the Gurdgieff Society. He promised that if we followed his leadership, we'd all be in something like the promise land. But it was a land grab for personal power. That night a young woman who had come with her newly converted boyfriend confessed to being pregnant and wondering what she should do. Without hesitation, this new guru said "Have it." And that was that. Wow. Let a total stranger make a decision like that for you? Not *moi*. But we would go to these gatherings, me out of curiosity, Lee because Raphael had convinced him he was Lee's intellectual equal and if Lee stuck "with it" whatever "it" was, he'd have all of his life in order.

Before long, Raphael was getting his following to do things like construct his house, help with his gaggle of kids, in general lead the sacred life by doing what he referred to as "the work." The work was always a project like tilling his garden, plastering his house, things of that nature. He wanted to create "an environment that would bond people together." I called it the Tom Sawyer Syndrome. I wouldn't do it. Even though I liked the company of those other people, I knew he was going to extract his pound of flesh, take us to the cleaners. I refused to go back to the meetings and would never attend one of his so-called social gatherings. It took me a while to see how many Raphaels there were in New Mexico. They came in every shape, size and lineage.

Most likely they would eventually run for government positions. Many years later I watched the full spectrum of this leadership as it grew first in San Francisco, then in Guyana. The leader at the time was a clean-hearted man called to serve, named Jim Jones.

Even Jerry had doubts about some of the aura-balancing people who started showing up at the bar. There was a young woman named Lola Lee and I found particularly scummy. We'd seen her at the flea market with a person who appeared to be her son. A friend of mine who I met at belly dancing told me it was her husband. Lola had deep raccoon coloring and sharp teeth. She reportedly had visions from Mary Magdalen and Isis, but I wasn't clear if it was at the same time. I saw her in a booth one Saturday at the flea market holding sessions for only twenty-five dollars a pop. Her booth was draped in exotic cloths and her husband stood outside in a cheesy-looking sombrero covered with spangles, the kind sold on the streets of Juarez. Lola claimed to be an expert on the Mayan people. I chatted with her a bit at the bar one night discovering she knew nothing about the people and especially about the Mayan calendar. That day at the market I watched elderly women go into her tent, the Indian bedspread closing behind them. I could only guess what baloney she was telling them as she invoked dead husbands and then purported to interpret dreams. I even overheard her tell someone she was a Jungian dream expert. This interested me as I had studied Jung, even considered going to the Institute in Switzerland. I asked her, "How do you like the system of archetypes?"

"It takes all types to make a world," she replied.

My favorite piece of nonsense had to do with sessions she was holding in Santa Fe on Canyon Road. I read about it in a flyer at the bar and finally tracked down someone who'd gone. Lola claimed to be in touch with an ancient crystal skull named Max who was "eons and eons old." For a twenty minute session at the price of forty bucks, a person could consult with Max through Lola who, because of his wisdom, had attained the status of an "awakened being."

The flyer was a bit astonishing. Here's what Lee and I read under the cone light at the bar: "I am no longer an old rock head hanging around inside a closet. I am now a Rock Star, presenting my message of unity around the world." Max, according to Lola, wasn't just old, he was "gadzillion-Atlantean" years old. According to the lore he was once a hunk of quart found in Guatemala and discovered by a Texan-Tibetan named Norbu Chen. Chen had a secretary named Jo Ann Parks and for a few eons Max sat in her closet (we guessed next to the mop and the bowling balls). Once Parks discovered the real truth about Max, how he came into being, she put him on tour making him the toast of the town. Although no one can account for how Max was made (no drill ever touched his sacred skull, nor did a jeweler's wheel or a diamond drill) no one could say how he was made. Nor could anyone account for Max's muffled wisdom. Somewhere on his fabulous path a person guessed the real truth of Max: he came directly from Atlantis. There were accounts of the secretary working along (much like Nixon's secretary) in an oblivious state when she heard a voice in the closet. "Let me outta here," said the magnificent being. And she did. How this precious piece of history fell into Lola's hands was never explained, just that she was the temporary guardian, knowing one day he would pass to another "avatar." But Lola promised the following from one of her interpretative sessions with Max: focused energy, reflected energy, attuned energy, transformation of all kind, amplification (what did that mean?) and an ability to transmit energy. Of course no one ever heard Max, but those who sat with him in silence came away in awe.

I chose a very different path from "the work," which seemed totally based on guilt and to some degree terror. I was sure I could learn to balance an aura if l wanted to. I certainly had psychic abilities but used them for things like grocery shopping after a dreadful event one weekend in Alabama. I had been partying for a weekend with friends and a few guys from Princeton showed up. It was refreshing to have a weekend with a fellow who was reading, taking interesting courses and liked art. And so the weekend became one long party. The night before these guys were slated to leave we drove to a restaurant out of town. As we passed over a bridge I asked them if they would remember what to do if they were in a V.W. bug and it crashed into a river. Everyone took this on as an interesting journey on being aware at the moment of death. The fellow I was with said he'd just sit there and watch the water swirl around him. He wouldn't remember that a V.W. is one vehicle that could be stabilized if it fell into say, a river. It could float.

After his comment the group became silent and uncomfortable and someone told me to "lighten up." I said I really didn't know why I brought that up, I didn't want to be a wet blanket, so to speak.

The next day as the boys were on their way back to Princeton, the large clunker car they were driving broke down and they were forced to return to Tuscaloosa and rent another car: a V.W. bug. As they crossed the bridge, it gave way. Everyone got out but my date. I was not allowed in the hospital rooms. Several friends actively avoided me and I felt the shadow of their gossip. After that I mostly kept my thoughts and premonitions to myself. As events, horrific ones, unfurled in my life I discovered I didn't always get the message on time. The muse in charge of timely intervention has her own idea of when to show up.

One day a friend who lived close by with a daughter the same age as Lilah dropped over. She looked around at our rented hovel house and declared I needed to get away once in a while. She whisked me off to Santa Fe, down Canyon Road to the adobe home of a woman named Lynn. Lynn had constructed a mud hogan attached to her house. Lynn had decided to jettison anything in her house that worked electrically like vacuum cleaner, blender, toaster, etc. She used a push broom instead of a vacuum, chopped everything by hand instead of whirring it in a machine and there was no television there, not even a radio.

Each Thursday we sat in the round room hung with rugs and Native American tapestry, smelling of pinon and candles. That was it. In silence we just sat quietly and settled into the earth like our dead adobe field. Once we washed rocks in the warm winter sun. Another day we washed feet. Everything we did was perfectly ordinary, simple and silent. No lectures about bonding. No scrubbing her floors to make us better people. No power games. I only knew Lynn's name and, of course, my friend, Sarah.

Sometimes at the end of our silence someone would read a passage. I was almost moved to tears by a Neruda quote: "Give me silence, water, hope. Give me struggle, iron, volcanoes."

For almost two hours, getting to Santa Fe, sitting and returning home, connected me to something in my core I'd been thirsting for. And Lynn maintained the "it" had no name. But this practice became a habit with me, giving me the kind of centering I badly needed in a life filled with chaos. On Thursdays I was let out of building jail. For the entire day I didn't mention the word rebar, cement, posthole diggers or trowels. One day, after a member had read a particularly poignant piece, I asked Sarah on the way home if she knew his name.

"Him? I think it's Alan Watts."

The music of our era had become more political than psychedelic groups like The Doors. Joanie Mitchell, for example, sang about the shrinking land, "pave paradise, put up a parking lot." We could see that happening with our own eyes glancing at disappearing mesas. If we could have done so, we'd have pulled the wagons together and formed a new society to protect ourselves against people like Nixon who wanted to pin long hairs down like Gulliver. No doubt we appeared to be out-laws to the likes of the conservative politicians. We wanted to make a stand against political corruption. The business world, the banks and insurance companies, were tainted with greed. Oil spills were leaking all over the globe. The word "alternative" now meant more than being zonked and good vibes, we wanted authenticity in our government, our elected officials. Finally Earth Shoes and hefty women were in fash-ion, pushing out the pill box hat ladies.

I was beginning to worry about the state of literature in my life. First, I didn't have time to read. I had started a book called "The Sot Weed Factor" and lost my place four different times. It wasn't that the book was boring, I just didn't have the time.

It appeared that the most popular book around was something called "Jonathan Livingston Seagull." To us it seemed ridiculously in-sipid. Even Nixon quoted it. There was talk at the bar of using the seagull on the 4th of July float. As the stony vision grew, they imagined a gigantic Jonathan trying to teach Evel Knievel to "soar." The ideas were funny, but too hard to put together. It was the rocket thing Evel rode in his farewell jump over Snake River Canyon that would eat up the budget. Someone suggested it wouldn't be a complete float unless there was a good load of poop. Then the discussion veered to where the poop should go: on Evel's head? How about on Jonathan's head, he's full o' crap? Over the booths that night, float ideas loomed large, but carrying through with the papier mache and chicken wire part of the project we all knew, would never happened.

The idea arose much later the bar should make a bust of Nixon saying "I'm not a crook." This would be easier to make as there were so many plastic masks of Nixon around they could glue it onto a man-nequin. Someone else commented on the flatness of a float anyone could make, it didn't show the bar's ingenuity. Then the idea was intro-duced of enhancing Nixon's face by pin pricking the mask and let sweat dribble down. Waste of water someone else said. Most of the creativity petered out before dawn. Still there was the worrisome challenge of what symbol would represent the bar on the Fourth of July parade.

In truth there were some closet Evel fans lurking around the village. A group of people from Santa Fe had been inspired to follow Evel to Twin Falls, Idaho, to watch his famous last jump. With them went bets. Most people bet the canyon would win. It was 540 feet deep. But Evel was one of the last heroes, like a redneck John Wayne. He was a tobacco-chewing, good old boy boozer; a braggart, and reminded folks a bit of Elvis. Jerry said he was *the* last American hero, a man who kept his word. "Probably the person who inspired the leisure suit."

The leisure suit was getting to be big fashion in Bernalillo. Even the most macho types could be seen wearing them in pastel colors; they resembled big Easter eggs. Once Morgan pointed to a particularly large man wearing a green leisure suit. "Look. Humpty Dumpty."

The most popular book around, besides Jonathan "Livingston Seagull" was the "Whole Earth Catalog." I remember seeing its fundamentals written on the wall at the health food co-op:

Everything's connected to everything;

Everything's got to go somewhere;

There's no such thing as a free lunch.

Amen.

Women were often excluded in Native American ceremonies. As powerful as they were, they didn't seem to fight the "Squaw, your place is home in the tee pee" mandate. But the women I met in New Mexico were a different brand of female. They took great pride in their house-building abilities while strumming instruments, nursing babies, throwing pots or weaving. We were the spiders in charge. In our area there became a fad that intrigued me: belly dancing. I remembered the women from Morocco, their spinning and ululating, so I joined a group. There was a sense of something deep and bonding to dance with a group of women who actually liked, celebrated, their protruding guts. One woman who'd given birth four times had something like a mandala scar on her belly. A new ritual began: Friday night belly dancing. Women danced, men drummed. The women were the center stage, twirling and gyrating, children running amok, climbing in and out of the home where we danced, another work-in- progress. Our children grew up thinking everybody lived in the equivalent of an archeological dig with living rooms often strewn with plaster bags, trowels and spackling compound. It was a far cry from my proper New Orleans upbringing. Here, all was wild and surprising, Annie Oakley, Wild Bill Hickup, as the kids called him--legends of the West. One New Mexican friend told me one Christmas she was given a doll and a rifle. I kept having a vision of her throwing the doll in the air, then pulling the trigger as if she were skeet shooting, splattering the doll all over the mesa. This place we landed fed my deep sense of irony. I liked that.

As soon as Morgan could hold a crayon, he was drawing pictures. He had a fierce imagination drawing Rube Goldberg driving machines with swimming pools dangling off, and multiple steering columns. We had a friend who had made a replica of the highway on the hood of his jalopy. From the vantage point of the steering wheel, you could see a plastic car driving down a painted highway complete with tiny sponge trees.

I figured this replica of a highway and car staying on the straight and narrow was his best way of navigating home. Morgan was fascinated with this set up and wanted us to glue a car to our hood as well.

Instead he drew fantasy cars he called "quality cars." I expect because we had such beat-up vehicles and lived such a Spartan life, his dreams included living in a motel, eating food from McDonalds and driving a car with a little class. Living on a road like ours tended to take the umph out of a car. The roads were either washboard rutted or so muddy we'd slide all over the hills. At one point we did own a Volvo station wagon we'd bought in Europe and brought back to the states. I loved the heft of that car and its demise was a speed bump in our life.

One weekend in spring a friend came to visit with another friend in tow. This was beginning to be a regular event. I didn't know until we'd settled into a booth at the Thunderbird the gent, the friend of the friend, in question wasn't really a friend, he had hitched the ride. But by the time I heard we had yet another drifter under our roof, he was gone. In our car. When folks disappeared from the bar it was usually to go out and have a smoke behind the building, or ingest a few pills. But this guy was gone for hours. It was nearly closing time, many beers emptied and stories of building hassles running out. This guy showed up with the police. He wasn't cuffed, but he had a certain hangdog look to him as he walked across the wooden bar floor. Police showing up at the bar was reason for just about everyone to scramble, flush their contraband or get under a table.

He addressed Lee. "Sorry, man. I totaled your car."

"That's not possible," I said. "Our car's in the parking lot."

Then I saw the look on Lee's face. "You loaned this scum bag our car?"

"He needed to get something back at the house."

"That wouldn't have to do with drugs, would it?" I asked them both.

He took off the next day promising to send us some cash. Right. To say things got rather tense at our house would be to ask if Elizabeth Taylor is a virgin. I'm not sure what the guy was "using" but I suspected peyote, the drug of choice at the time. Lee and I had argued many times about using at parties and what not. I knew I'd be driving home, but that meant I had to curb my wine. The car episode was a timeline blip in our lives.

There had been so many accidents on our roads, the altars alongside the highways, the *descansos,* were testaments to alcohol, drugs and chance. Once in Truchas, we passed a graveyard with a gigantic motorcycle as a grave marker. I imagine what might have been inscribed on the stone: He died doing what he loved best, or God Bless Harley. Jerry often talked about the way he had to dodge Indians driving on the wrong side of the highway coming back from a place near Jemez called Rosie's Cantina. "Fuckers can't hold their booze," he said, verifying the rumor we had heard when we moved to New Mexico.

People, like the one who trashed our car, always seemed to walk away unscathed, leaving the car and most likely other people flattened on the roadside.

Many years later I happened to watch a television game show. Who should appear but the guy who totaled our car, posing as a wine taster from California. And he won. Enough to pay us back for the damage he'd caused in our life. But trying to get a network to shake out the name and particulars of a contestant is like trying to make the New Mexican Bell South Telephone Company put in your phone lines.

We bought a Scout. A sturdy stripped-down car that took to the hills like a champ, but our insurance covered the barest necessities, no rugs, no radio. I was glad to have seats. But it could haul cement bags, which I had to buy at least twice a week.

One gusty spring day while I was in Bernalillo, it threw a rod. We ended up looking at a vehicle even Zeke wouldn't buy, a beat-up truck with close to bald tires. It only lasted six months and broke down on the freeway. When we went to get it towed the next day the entire thing had been stripped down, tires gone, everything inside worth stealing most likely being sold at the Flea Market on Fourth Street.

"What'd you expect, man?" someone said at the bar as we recounted our tale of woe. "Cars don't get repaired out here. They just get ditched."

The bar wasn't exactly a Mecca of compassion. For every horror story like ours, someone could match it with worse. It was spring and everyone was getting light-headed from the surge of heat and sunshine. It was bar-b-que time in the parking lot of the bar. Giant metal containers were transformed into bar-b-que pits. Most were painted silver, I suspected because they'd been ripped off from some oil company or garage. I distrusted eating food off a grill that had a funny metallic smell, so we stuck to the tabouli and the ubiquitous watermelon.

The guys liked these events best because all the women were dancing mostly bare breasted. Suddenly we saw how white we'd become over winter. I felt like a piece of abalone out there dancing with the kids to a not-very-good local band. These events were also opportunities for folks to sell the wares they'd been working on all winter whilst held up in their lairs against the ice and snow. There were some nice weavings, lots of macramé, and art none of us could afford to buy. We had a preponderance of talented artists in our area, but most had to go to Santa Fe to make a sale. The hand-made huaraches using tire treads as soles were always the hottest items, even though they produced great blisters for a few weeks. Next to the shoes, tie-dyed shirts and skirts were still in fashion. And now, the new fad for belly button piercing made the drop-waist garments even more appealing.

There was a fellow who lived alone up the canyon who called himself Titus. Lee and I wondered if he'd read the play *Titus Andronicus,* but since he only blew air through his harmonica it was hard to have a conversation with him. His incessant honking made me think of a raspy iron lung. He reminded me of people found in caves, raised by wolves or coyotes. Most of the Thunderbird folks thought his name was Tight Ass. His garment of choice was a leather loin cloth. This garment was particularly interesting when the spring winds picked up. We never knew when or where he'd show up: school plays, Ditch Day or the spring flings in the parking lot. One thing for sure, Lilah hated this guy. Her sensibilities were offended, even at this young age, and she'd often pitch a pebble at his butt if she thought we weren't looking. Years later he showed up at a ballet class held in the village. Lilah said she wouldn't go to class if he were present forcing a showdown with the teacher who happened to be his friend. Lilah won. Score one for my daughter.

The Scout had been our main vehicle for transporting tiles from Juarez, Mexico We'd made several trips down there loading up on Talavera tiles, sinks and pottery. But before we took off for Juarez, we'd gone up the mountains for a picnic. The spring winds weren't as pronounced in the mountains. Lilah said it was harder for the wind to find us up there where it couldn't show off so much. She was referring to the way the dust dervished around the mesas making a cyclone of dirt and garbage. We were blindfolded by dust.

On the way to the stream, one of our children had fouled the nest and the scent from their diapers was overwhelming. Our friend Johnny, crammed into the back seat with them said he had to stop and get fresh air. I was too frugal to throw away a good cloth diaper. I figured with two babies in diapers I could probably hit my dotage with dusting cloths from their pre-underpants phase. We stopped in a shady spot, Johnny smoking and mumbling to himself about the stench in the back seat. Soiled diapers were normal to me, I no longer took notice of their malodorous nature, like dog owners unaware of the doggy odor in their homes. And I refused to throw a good diaper away.

Even when we rinsed it in the stream, it carried a bouquet. I was struck with what I thought was a brilliant idea. Put the offensive diaper in the hubcap. Sure, why not? Everyone would win. I wouldn't have to throw it out, Johnny didn't heave in the back seat. The day unfolded pleasantly.

Flash forward. We are leaving Mexico loaded with not just tiles, but pottery and *objects* d'arte. Going to Juarez to buy supplies gave us a day away from the building process and a little romantic time in a motel. I didn't have the cash to call the home to check on the children, so perforce, they were out of sight. Out of mind.

We pulled into the little parking area in customs, me not paying much attention to the people going over our car with mirrors, dogs sniffing our tires. We were longhairs and used to being stopped by the authorities. Our greatest fear was called "the cavity search," which made me think of Thanksgiving. I had a friend undergo such an invasion. It was worth the effort to get a haircut and where a shirt waist dress to avoid such a thing.

I was filing my nails, ignoring the customs officers trying to look blase, when I remembered something. Something about a diaper. But the dogs were already onto it and the officer was prying off our hubcap with the forgotten diaper hidden inside.

Before long a caucus had formed around the tire as they poked at what they were sure was a big drug bust. Lee and I didn't say anything as we tried to think of how we would explain the entire situation to the authorities, in English. They were actually sniffing my child's diaper. I wanted to say, "Don't taste it, please." But we were hauled into a cubicle to explain just what the substance was. The word was simple "caca."

"Caca, senora?"

"Straight, pure, unadulterated caca, direct from my child to your table."

It took hours to get out of there and I reckoned it would be our last buying trip for some time. I was right about that.

While we were delayed at the border, our children had spent a few days with a lackadaisical sitter in Corrales. I felt okay about her as we'd only be gone a day and a half and her mother was going to check in regularly. When we returned I sat down to talk to the kids and show them some silly toys I'd bought for them. A straw tube with open ends, insert two fingers and you can't get either out until you relax. I was looking over Morgan's new drawings and I saw one with a new motif.

"What's that?" I asked.

"A flying hamburger."

"Did you go out for a hamburger?" I'd left their food, cooked in the frig; eggplant, lasagna, posole. No hamburger.

"No." He kept drawing circular discs that looked strangely like spaceships. "Did you see a flying hamburger?"

"Yes."

"Where?"

He pointed to the mesa outside the window. "Did you see it more than one time?"

"Yes."

"Every day?" He looked up at me as if I were an idiot, as if to say *of course.*

Weird things had been happening that year, inexplicable things. We'd heard the stories of the UFOs cited as early as the forties. Everyone seemed to know the buzz word "Roswell." There were still plenty of people around us who still swore to have seen odd lights in the sky. Like light bulbs popping, one person said. Balls of fire, circular discs, yellow flashes, silver-colored discs that zigged and zagged across the sky, sometimes hovering, then shooting off.

Stories about aliens were like yeti sightings; everyone who went into the mountains was sure they'd seen a yeti out of the comer of their eye. Yeti sightings seemed to be most plentiful in the forests where the foliage helped disguise the creature; something akin to a Disney heroine being saved from evil forces by birds and small animals.

In the yeti retelling stories at the bar, the mention of dope only came in as a coda to the tale. What gave the original alien stories credibility to me were the old newspaper reports about farmers and ranchers sitting on their porches during a storm. This wasn't a group of dopers, just plain old folk palavering in the evening. Each one interviewed reported hearing an enormous sound, like an explosion. They said they could tell it wasn't thunder, it sounded different. One farmer saddled up and went to look for the source of the sound and exploding light. According to the story in the papers, he discovered some odd wreckage. The metal, according to the legend, wasn't from this earth. It looked like foil but was stronger, and more pliable.

Another account said they'd actually seen odd folk, aliens, with big heads, no hair and slanted eyes. Things got more interesting when one of the farmers picked up a piece of the wreckage and took it home. Later, so the story goes, he was muscled by the military to hand the stuff over and keep his mouth shut. Hmmm. The man, many years later, swore it was not a weather balloon, the story the government tried to press on the public at large. It was not a radar tracking device. The man who discovered this inexplicable material also found odd wood with symbols on it looking like hieroglyphs. The army confiscated all of the debris and the farmer got mighty quiet.

Jerry believed all of this and kept the old moldy papers in his free form. I was over there borrowing a pair of pliers when I saw the papers stuck to a cork board, the one that went missing from the second-grade classroom in the Village. He'd circled the poignant parts of the article, the "inexplicable material," with a red marker.

I had a moment to get some more detail of the interior of the free form as he looked around for the pliers. Faded paper dolls from Mexico with the name "Lola" painted on them lined one of the shelves carved out of the wall. The Lola dolls were covered with spangles, their heads shaped in such a way I imagined the creator was thinking about constructing a male doll, then turned the Elvis-like head into a female's softer, more alluring shape.

I don't know who was making the models of small cars and plastic planes next to what was referred to as the sink. I recognized the projects from kits my brother used to put together as a child. Was there a child in the freeform nobody knew about? Perhaps Jerry's passion for playing with some idea spurred him into making a model. A weathered kite was tied high up near the hub caps in the "free form" and made a ghostly sound when the wind whistled through the house.

Jerry had a favorite chicken in the barnyard he liked to stroke named Jon-Jon. I assumed the fowl was named after the President's son. But I was wrong. Jon-Jon was named after a character in a book, the takeoff on the seagull book entitled "Jonathan Segal Chicken" about a Jewish super chicken who took on the world.

Sometimes he'd toss the chicken up in the air saying things like "Forgive the flock man." Or "Be yourself, Dude." Once he asked me if I'd ever seen a chicken stoned. He regularly blew smoke in his cat's ears and watched the poor creature try and navigate the already difficult tilting of the free form structure. A stoned chicken had no appeal for me.

Jerry seemed to be getting on better with our kids. Once I saw him sitting on the cable spool overlooking the mesa, Morgan by his side. I imagined he was teaching Morgan to count in Spanish, the way he held his fingers up. As I got closer I saw, with astonishment, he was sticking pins in his finger.
"See Dude," he said to Morgan, "makes your skin tougher."
"Doesn't that hurt?"
"Not anymore," Jerry answered.

He invited the kids over to feed the chickens. This seemed like a nice barnyard gesture so I asked him what he fed his flock.
"Table scraps," he replied. "They really dig fried chicken."

I had a chance to find out more about his Donner Party fare one day at sunset. "What's up with feeding Jon-Jon Kentucky fried?" "Dig it. All animals need to get flinty, man. Like the dope I grow. The more I torture it, the better the smoke."
"What about karma?" I asked.
"Chickens are highly evolved; they're already at the top of the food chain, spiritually speaking." He stroked Jon-Jon the way a person pets a cat.
"Spiritually speaking," I echoed.

Meanwhile back in alien folklore, sightings had been reported all over New Mexico.

A flying disc over Roswell apparently rolled over many times, enough to give the bystander a closer look at the phenomena. Someone near White Sands even got a snapshot of something about 300 feet in diameter traveling at speeds of 2,000 miles an hour. (How did they clock that?) The government's broken record response all over the state was that what they'd seen was a weather balloon. But the rumors never died and people had seen what they had seen. As one man recounted, "I saw what I saw."

The most intriguing and lasting account dated back to 1964 in Socorro. A couple outside the town of Socorro were having car difficulty one night. When the car stopped, they got out to look under the hood. Never seen or heard from again.

Incident #2. A family driving a green Cadillac were heading south from Colorado. An oval-shaped object whizzed over their car so close it clipped their antenna. The object whisked over the horizon in a split second leaving the family bewildered. They told their story to a patrol officer who had just been investigating a loud explosion noise near a facility that housed dynamite. According to the tale, the officer had actually witnessed a white metal object in the arroyo. This guy not only saw the object, but swears he saw two smallish figures near it. When he moved closer to them, they disappeared. Before that, however, the officer stated he saw a weird red insignia on the side of the "craft." When he closed in on the object, a bright blue light or flame burst causing a huge roar, loud enough for him to hit the ground, then it flew away.

Other people in the Socorro area called in that same night reporting noise and lights similar to what the others had experienced. But what was interesting about this tale was the aftermath. When they examined the area the next day, it was reported they found four depressions in the dirt in a quadrangular pattern. They reckoned that something enormous had been pushed into the earth by a jumbo weight.

Once the military got involved, even firsthand accounts got hazy. One man apparently lifted a piece of evidence and took it home with him: a bit of fractured stone with tiny specks and slivers. His proof was quickly taken to a lab, discounted and discredited by a UFO debunker. These stories still floated about the Thunderbird Bar like dust motes.

At each telling a new and unheard detail revealed the belief the government was trying to cover up what might be an alien invasion. Whatever Morgan kept drawing, it didn't frighten him. That was comforting because more odd UFO stories arose after a series of cattle mutilations were reported nearby. Lee suggested the incisions, the surgery, might have something to do with my father experimenting on some new procedures.

But the mutilations spawned the paranoia that the government was watching us, studying our habits. Folks were more afraid of the politicians than they were of aliens.

Nights in New Mexico were dazzling with great nets of stars. It made me feel like the universe was showing herself in ways that could not be ignored. It was possible with all the twinkling stars and planets to believe life, other than that which we knew, was closer than we thought.

The cattle mutilations during the decade we lived there had a pernicious feel. Unlike the episodes involving friendly little elf-like people sited in Socorro, these events happening close by had a gruesome edge, and all of the fingerprints were alike.

Animals killed at night had their sexual organs, tongues, udders and rectums removed by sharp instruments. Sometimes the eyes and lips were also removed. The startling fact was there was no sign of blood. There were never footprints, tire marks or disturbances around the animal's body. Not even evidence that coyotes had attacked the animal. In conjunction with these weird occurrences, there were more reports about odd flying objects, flashes of light and loud unidentifiable noises. These things weren't just happening in New Mexico; the paper reported cattle mutilations all over Colorado as well. There were rumors at the bar that all of this work was a result of left-over Nazis who lived underground and were being fed and kept alive by rednecks and a secret society of Republicans.

I thought the idea of the underground railway run by deranged Republicans very inventive.

Apparently these mutilation events weren't just recent, but had continued over a period of as much as ten years totaling thousands of mutilated cattle and horses. When farmers and ranchers were hit hard by events like these, they started to call senators and the like.

Farmers and ranchers wanted to believe in predators, but where we lived it was all about aliens. Then stories surfaced that the mutilations were pranks. I knew it was just a matter of time before all the longhairs would be blamed for these odd occurrences. But frankly, I didn't know a single hippie who could perform the kind of surgery on these animals without leaving a trace. One person reported the skin on his cattle had been peeled back like a can of sardines. All I could think of was the guy who self-lobotomized himself at the bar.

A friend of ours who lived in a commune in southern Colorado became obsessed with the cattle mutilations. He carried on extensive research, interviews and speculation. He was leaning towards "the government is poisoning us" theory. It wasn't long before the hypothesis of cultists emerged as a way of explaining these events. The people in our area, were sure they were the target of suspicion, put forth a theory that the government had been messing with our brains and used the cattle as barometers. "It's a mind shaft, man," Jerry told us while sucking on a joint. "Like either it's the government or aliens. I'd rather have the aliens." He gazed skyward. "Like the Indians don't let the feds on their land. Them Indians know when the sky folks are coming down. Like they leave them alone."

No matter what, something undeniable was happening. When I looked up in the sky or saw any of Morgan's drawings of f\flying hamburgers, I got an uneasy feeling. That feeling was a nudge to get out of Dodge. But, I ignored it until it came way too close.

The alien stories fed into one of the larger mysteries of New Mexico: what had become of the Anasazi Indians? Some said they were blighted off the earth by God, the Spider Woman, because their time was up. Other explanations I heard explained their disappearance as a volcanic explosion, a meteor blast, while others indicated it might have been due to tooth decay (no floss?) but the most prevalent story in our area named drought as the cause.

Morgan got me to tell him the story of the evaporated tribe over and over.

"Maybe they went underground," he said. "Maybe they're still there watching until they think it's safe to come out."

I'd showed the kids a photograph of Indians descending into an underground kiva.

The idea of a secret subterranean place became a theme in games with Morgan and Lilah's friends. Over and over we warned them not to go digging around the culverts, and especially not to go near the holes in the hillside that looked like caves. Robert Creeley's son had been killed when an arroyo like that collapsed on him.

We visited the great ruins at Chaco Canyon, seeing what must have been an advanced civilization built in the tenth century. I wasn't prepared for the highly structured nature of this khaki-colored ruin, the kivas, the buildings organized with purpose and thought, but no written history to explain it all. There was a stone building that had masonry so tightly packed it resembled something from the Museum of Modern Art. Monumental walls. The silence of the place was deafening. But what interested me as much as the architecture was the building known as the The Great House, designed to register a lunar event that happened only once in every 18 years known as a lunar standstill. This civilization had an observatory.

In many ways it reminded me of the rock structures at StoneHenge. But here, two enormous sandstone frames kept the moon in view during the two or three nights of this odd event where the moon takes a rare side trip and appears to rise and fall at the same place.

Best as I could understand it, for two or three consecutive nights. Along with a confusing explanation in our guidebook was the fact that at the moment the moon appeared between these two spires, coyotes began to howl, then once the moon changed its position, frozen silence. A lunar astigmatism?

The Anasazi civilization spread nearly a hundred thousand miles. I've seen aerial photographs that looked like crude road maps in all directions. Their telecommunications: smoke signals from mesa to mesa. Wherever they went, their stamp still lives in the Southwest pueblos. Some of the most ancient pueblos like Acoma and Zuni are thought to be direct lineage of these amazing people who reportedly were the creators of beautiful pots and woven baskets.

But the prevailing story at the bar was that the Anasazi had become cannibals.

At the Thunderbird recorded history often took on a macabre twist and had little to do with known facts. No matter what the fables were, their disappearance haunts the Southwest the way that the disappearance of Virginia Dare from America haunts our history books. The first child born in America, on American soil, it is said, was Virginia Dare.

Today there are so many folks claiming to be "kin" to Virginia Dare she has taken on mythical proportions as progenitor. And like Virginia Dare, so many tribes, such as the Navajo, claim to be part of the offspring of the Anasazi. I didn't doubt it; Spider Woman gave these people the gift of creativity. In the Southwest such a gift never dies. And maybe an alien saucer did scoop them up. That's what Jerry believed. He should have known, his own cave was a warren of petroglyphs and paint-by-number inspirations. But one of the greatest inspirations of Chaco Canyon was this: after about a thousand years the buildings were still standing. This gave me great hope about our own house- in progress.

Jerry and I were sitting on a stack of melting adobes looking in the direction of the Jemez Mountains. "Aliens all the hope we got left," Jerry said, his eye watering up.

His sentimental reaction made me wonder if he was going soft in the head, but then I remembered the afternoon when he drove up with Lilah in the front seat.

Lilah's friend's mother was supposed to have dropped her off at our home. Instead, she let her off in front of the stuffed donkey house. From there Lilah trudged on home but stopped short when she heard, then saw a rattler stretched across the road.

At that moment Jerry drove up and told Lilah to get into the front seat. Then Jerry rolled over the snake, not just once, but three times. Later, as Lilah recounted the incident she said, "Jerry said "Have a nice life, dude."

Later he told me this was his method of accelerating karma:

A new commune cropped up near us. Over the years they'd sprouted like mushrooms in the Southwest out on the bumpy roads the school bus couldn't navigate. They showed up in clumps en route to the warm springs in Jemez, or to load up bulk foods at the newly begun food co-op on Fourth Street.

I told Lee we should be on the National Registry for Communes. But this one, too close to our home, wasn't organized like the Ant Farm in Colorado; it was more like a half-way house. Stray children wandered around the hillside like lost goats.

One little boy in particular, found his way to our house like a stray dog. His full-blown name was Zuzax after the town where the mother gave birth on the side of the road.

"I never was good at counting," she told us with a shrug. Figured he'd be coming in Spring. Dead of winter in a snowstorm. Zuzax was quickly nicknamed Zax, much easier for everyone to say. He was a profoundly sad little boy with hair every which way and a speech impediment that made everything he said difficult to understand.

Quite often he showed up in our kitchen staring at a jar of peanut butter, running one of Morgan's trucks up and down the table. I always fed him at least one meal, but made him bathe before he ate.

His hair was matted and his ears distressingly dirty. He had funny scabs and marks that made me wonder about his home life. I felt uneasy going to his house. People that looked drugged drifted in and out of their plywood and tent home a mesa away from us.

The mother had gotten into what she called "paint therapy." I thought that meant she was getting help from a therapist or at least a social worker.

Once when I brought Zax home she was working on a paint-by-number canvas, but she was so stoned she'd gotten the colors and numbers mixed up so the dog she was working on had purple eyes.

She hardly looked up when Zax and I came into their tent. Even though it was warm she wore layers of sweaters and jackets and a rainbow-colored yarn hat I'd seen Zax wearing as well.

"I think he has a fever," I told her that day.

"Yeah?"

"Do you have a thermometer?"

"I'll take him to the emergency room," she said adding, "when my old man gets back."

'He's pretty hot. Might be an infection."

"I got herbs. Cool squaw at the flea market sold them to me."

I left them, wanting to take Zax down to our doctor in town.

"Don't interfere," Lee said.

"Is it interference? That little boy needs medical attention. I have creepy feelings about what's going on down there. All those scruffy dogs scare me. No running water. It makes Jerry's place look like a New York high-rise."

About a week later I happened to look out the window, shocked to see Zax in our courtyard. He was lying on his side biting the tire on Morgan's bicycle. I went out and put my hand on his back to quiet him down. I thought he might be having a fit of some kind. Eventually he stopped and looked at me as if I weren't there. I began to suspect they were giving him drugs.

Several months later a social worker showed up at my door. Her questions were odd and indirect until she began asking about anything I'd noticed that seemed unusual. If she'd ever been to our part of the map, she would know that everything was unusual. Even I had lost track of what normal was.

"Unusual? That would be everything."

So I focused on things like the tire biting, the times he showed up hungry and not knowing where his mother had gone. She wrote it all down then left. We didn't see either mother or son after that. I always wondered where the little boy had landed. Any house with four walls would have been foreign to him. He was like a child discovered in a cave.

One evening at sunset as I washed dishes looking at the mountains, I thought of the last words from an old movie, *The Night of The Hunter,* when the elderly woman played by Lillian Gish looked straight into the camera and pronounced "God save the children."

The day we moved into the house the sky was Madonna cape blue. It was spring and the dust storms had just begun. This seemed a bad omen to me as I scurried to get everything together. Our move was disorganized, haphazard and all I could think of as we bumped along in a truck up our grooved road was a Conestoga wagon with pots and pans banging, hitting deep ruts, quilts dripping off the furniture, jostling and concussing all the way to our new home.

When we were told that once the walls are up, the roof is on your house, you are half done, I didn't believe them. I should have. We still had rooms needing plaster, tiles to be laid in bathrooms and kitchen, brick floors to be sealed and finished, staining on some of the newer vigas, and the list went on and on. And we had to put up a plywood barrier to the bedroom we would build in the future. We'd always planned on this room with its own fireplace and attached bath.

Our funds gave out. And so we nailed Beacon moving quilts over the temporary structure that would be the small entry to our one-day in-the-future bedroom. Even with the thick cloths, the wind whistled through the cracks. We were in. *Que Milagro.* We'd crossed the finish line. Were still breathing. Still married.

Within a week my washing machine was up and running, my clothesline strung. I pinned the diapers on the line watching the mesa, the headless volcano, Cabezon, the Jemez mountains as distant and mysterious as the High Atlas.

I practically needed a timer to be reminded to take clothes down from the line. If I left them too long, they hardened and became as stiff as cardboard. I could have carried them off like backdrops in a theatrical production. Inside the kitchen I tasted the water from our own deep well. Sweetwater.

During our building time I had decided that thirst was a kind of disease like alcoholism ... once you started to drink good water, you could never get enough. In front of me I toasted the mighty Sandias with a glass of the finest water I'd ever tasted. The Sandias, once considered intimidating, felt welcoming. Everything had changed. Smells had intensified, distances had become Kodachrome, and finally I quit looking for trees.

Anvil headed clouds bunched along the mountain tops. With no telephone in our house yet, we were constantly driving to town to use a pay phone. But the promise of the phone had made me heady with hopefulness. Each pay phone excursion gave me an excuse to go to the Bernalillo Mercantile, a place as bizarre as Morocco with Indian women dressed in crushed velvet blouses, heavy strings of turquoise jewelry and long black braids cascading down their backs. I thought perhaps they were from Santa Domingo Pueblo, but it didn't matter which pueblo they came from, they were dazzling in their array of colors and cloth.

Next door to the Merc, as we called it, an attached small store sold odd items, like old dry goods stores. But this store catered to the Indians. I stared at the wall of cubbyholes filled with bones, bells, shells, scarves and small bolts of velvet. Since I'd been to the corn dances at Santa Anna Pueblo, I could imagine the costumes reassembling with all the details of shelled ankles, gourds and the rattle of deer bones, even remembered the heartbeat sound of the drums. Just being there was a Proustian, pueblo flashback. Native Americans: New Mexico's most valuable natural resource.

Sometimes I studied rusted grocery carts left in the street, trying to decipher what Indians cooked inside their secret walls. Pork rinds seemed to be high on the list, beans, chile, and from the dairy counter, *carne adovado,* a ghastly bucket of pork marinated in red chile, giving the dish a distressing surgical look. Along the food aisle smeary plastic bags of herbs, the names written in Spanish, looked like lids of marijuana.

The glass counters in the there were grubby and lardy, children's smudgy fingerprints on everything. It was like being back in New Orleans in a corner grocery store in our neighborhood where everything was real, buckets of olives, cheese cut from large wheels, no packaging. The flooring was wooden and had squeaky boards reminding me of an old five and dime I frequented as a child.

That day I closed my eyes and guessed the description of the person behind me could tell whether he/she was wearing cowboy boots or the almost inaudible shuffle of moccasins. Some boots are easy to hear, especially those turquoise belt buckle types with silver and turquoise inherited from his father, not purchased in Santa Fe by his wife who draped herself in the big blue stones.

The Merc was also a favorite spot for the commune folks. They tried to out primitive the Native Americans with their bright blouses, strings of jewelry their children slung a la papoose on their backs, but they never got it authentically correct.

I was driving back home teaching the children to sing "The Big Rock Candy Mountain," and feeling lucky to live in a place on the earth so strange and compelling. The mesas and the mountains had cast a mighty a spell on me. Once I was eavesdropping at the post office and heard someone say, "All life comes from the mountains. Those mountains have the biggest ear to God."

It was no wonder they were worshipped by the Indians.

Sunset on the Sandias is a pink blush, then gone; we compared it to Alpen glow seen in the mountains of Italy: the Dolomites.

We waited for it each afternoon, as if it affirmed some pagan belief that because we'd seen the etymology of pink, the next day would arrive, the sun would push across the roof of the world and things would go on as usual. It was a view held by the Indians who believe their job is to move Father Sun across the sky. If the sons of the sun didn't fervently pray, all of the world would be plunged into darkness. I liked this idea, it reminded me of a scene from my favorite movie *Black Orpheus,* when the child picks up a guitar and plays it sitting on a wall looking over the roofs of the barrios in Rio. The little boy in the film had been told if he didn't play that song each morning before daybreak, the sun would not rise. This movie had special meaning for Lee and me. We'd seen it twelve times. And had bought the soundtrack, the guitar music we often hummed while we worked. It had a soft soothing effect. I hummed that theme from the movie that day as I dismounted my car and got the children and groceries out of the car.

I didn't have to push my door as I entered. It was already open. On the floor my black robe spread out like an outline in a crime scene. Everything seemed out of place, disorienting. It took me a long walk through into bedrooms, drawers opened and emptied to understand we'd been robbed. And because our locks hadn't been put on properly, all the thief had to do was give a little push, ransack and run. I was stunned. How did anyone find us so far out on this mesa? They had taken a risk, as there was only one way out of the mesa back to the highway.

I put the kids into the car and went back down to the pay phone next to the freeway to call the police. I tried explaining where we lived, not easy when you are so far off the map.

There are no immediate identifiable signs such as *next to the mailbox or first bridge on the right.* All I had for a description akin to "first stuffed donkey on the left." And then I added, "Jerry's free form." It was the free form that got their attention. They sure knew where that was.

"That the place that looks like a witch's hat?"

"Yep, I replied.

` "Those the folks that hid that fella who shot his wife? Who also took somebody's backhoe without permission."

"Look. I don't know about that. I do know I have an emergency here. Could you please come now? I have two small children. A break in. The thieves might be out in the brush somewhere."

Officer Pinot sauntered through the house with me, the children trailing, gaping at his leather holster, his spurred boots. He was quiet as we went from room to room, me showing him where our silver had been, my clothes, purses, and even a nice pair of shoes.

"No television. They must have got that."

"We don't own a television."

This was like saying we didn't eat chile.

He played with the wires to our aged KLH record player. Read a few titles from our bookshelves and ambled back to the kitchen.

"Where's your phone?" he asked.

I explained to him, in detail, how the phone company had stalled, then proposed no fee and we were still waiting.

He asked me how they got in. I told him there was no forced entry as our doors didn't lock properly. He glanced around the room at our old beams, our rustic furniture and our general look of aged, primitive hacienda. He shook his head.

I described the antique silver pieces that had been stolen, the initials from great grandparents scrolling the dishes and serving ware. It wasn't until that moment that I began to register the feeling of violation. I stared at the mountains as if they were somehow in collusion with the robbers. The day had gotten cloudier, making ominous manta ray shadows on the hills. Suddenly our cheery kitchen felt chilly and too big. I had to sit down.

"If I was you, Mrs. Johnson," he tipped his hat up slightly, "I'd get a gun."

"I don't want a gun."

"They know they didn't get everything. They'll be back."

"Great. I don't know how to use a gun. I hate weapons."

"You don't have a phone. I'd get that gun."

He wrote up his report and handed me a card with his name and phone number. I wanted to remind him how redundant it was to give me a phone number, but I felt exhausted and scared. What would I do if they came back and the children were home? I couldn't struggle with a gun with kids in the house. And I was pretty sure I couldn't use it. But I didn't want to test that out.

PART IV

A PLACE CHANGES completely in the space of an hour. I started thinking of how, in the event of an assault, to barricade myself in. Suddenly
all the space, large rooms and hallways, the design I'd been extolling
looked like a threat. I wanted to call in the troops, shut down the gates,
build an inner courtyard with a wall.

And now the light outside seemed over-bright and disorienting,
like walking out of a movie theater. And I started noticing all the icy
spots in the room. Places where a psychic would stop and palaver with
a spirit, perhaps.

There were too many portals into our home. No way to make it
safe, it was as open as a sieve. And I didn't want a gun.

When Lee came home I told him about what the officer had said.
We talked about it way into the night. Me trying to get past the idea of
a gun in the house. Lee trying to figure out how to close everything in.
We decided to hide anything of value in odd places like the fireplace,
up on the loft under the mattress for the rest of the silver flatware,
under the armoire for my jewelry. But all of the frantic hiding made us
more tense and in a few hours we'd already forgotten where we'd hidden what.

Lee knew how tense I'd become and suggested calming ways to ease
my fears. We'd take breaks and go for blue com tortilla lunches with
the kids even though it wasn't in our budget. At sunset we took long
walks in the arroyo. Finally, I quit looking up at our house wondering
if the burglars were in there pilfering. Although we didn't speak of the
break-in to the children they sensed somethimg big had happened and
became quieter, spending more time reading and building dirt houses
out back. I was torn between leaving the house and the possibility
of coming home to find someone still in there pilfering. I wanted to
batten down the hatches, boil oil and pour kerosene into bottles that
might be lit like Molotov cocktails, the way we'd seen the students
make them in the riots in Paris in 1968. Every knife in our kitchen had

the potential of being used on me. We went to a gun store in Bernalillo and bought a rifle. On the way home we passed Jerry who took the news of burglars with a grain of salt.

"That's what happens when you own stuff," he said sucking away on his joint. "Somebody always wants what you got." He thumped his finger against the door to his VW. "Want a smoke man? Chill you out."

"No." I spoke for both of us.

I was pretty disgusted with his cool disregard, but then we told him we'd just bought a rifle. He gave a low whistle. "Nothing scarier than a woman with a rifle. All you got to do, man, is just stand there with that sucker."

"Thanks for your vote of confidence," I said.

"See man, if you leave the place open like we do, nobody bothers you."

"Is that so?" Lee said.

As I went to sleep that night, I imagined I heard someone on the roof. I remembered the last time I'd used a rifle. I was ten. Daddy wanted me to learn to skeet shoot. All night long I heard his voice yelling, "pull, pull, pull." I remember my shoulder hurting from the kickback, seeing the clay pigeon splatter in the air when I finally hit one. I curled into a ball and considered putting everything we owned of value in our brick courtyard as if we were having a yard sale, but with a sign saying, "Take what you want and go away."

My fears were flamed when Officer Pinot returned in a week.

"We got some bad news for you, Mrs. Johnson."

"Go on."

"Lots of robberies. We got the description of the guy.

His name is Ricardo Ortega. A bad dude. Pretty sure this is his work."

"So are you going to patrol around the house?"

"Hey, this place is pretty remote." I remember the way he said "pretty" it was elongated like preeeeeeety remote. My confidence level crashed. I felt like I had a bag of sand in my stomach that had just been slit. And I wondered if he was going to offer up what he meant by "bad dude," and moreover, did I really want the thief's job description. If I knew the kind of crimes he'd committed, it would be like giving the guy scenery, a backdrop and music for an opening scene. My imagination was already going wild. I didn't need a single new detail. The threat of being physically attacked had jerked me awake. And I kept putting off practicing with the rifle. It might call down bad stuff. I needed some kind of prayer. Voo Doo. Rosary. Mantra. And soon.

Weeks later my sister came to visit from Colorado. We caught up on her children, life in Boulder and gossip about New Orleans. I didn't want to dwell on what had happened, my breath got short each time I told someone and I felt my heart pound. I could not stay on alert forever, it was getting to me. The expression, "Watch your back," haunted me.

Sometime in the afternoon she wanted to touch base with her kids in Boulder, and so she and Lee and our children went down to Bernalillo to make a pay phone call. I was sitting in the zome living room watching a knife of light slice across the *Sandias,* then watched it slide onto our oxide red earthen floor. That's when I heard Lee and the family drive back. I went into the kitchen wondering what they'd forgotten. But it wasn't them. It was a threesome, young Chicano adults who got out of a white car that nearly dragged the ground. Instantly, I knew the robbers had returned. I ran to the door and bolted it with the new lock we'd installed. I looked at the broom closet where the rifle was stored. I didn't want to touch the thing. Besides it wasn't loaded. Someone jokingly said that accidents only happen with guns that are "unloaded."

They were at our threshold when I spoke. "What do you want?"

They stopped. Pulled into a group, then one stepped forward. "We're looking for someone named Terry."

I could hardly breathe. I had to pee so bad my bladder hurt. I spoke without thinking. "No you're not."

The guy stepped backwards again and they stood in our brick courtyard in a huddle, like the players in a football game figuring out their strategy. I moved towards the sink so I could see how they were going to configure. My car was on the other side of theirs. I couldn't get to it. If they divided, they'd conquer. And so many ways to get in. Our back door, the bathroom windows, the bedroom windows, the flimsy plywood partition we'd put up when had to stop building, closing up the hallway to the third bedroom that one day would be built. I was in the middle of a house of cards.

Then I had to consider the biggest fear, the sound of a discharging rifle. I looked straight out at the *Sandias,* recalled the words about how all life comes from the mountain. I didn't want to close my eyes as I might not see one of the thieves darting around the back of the house. *Please,* I asked the mountains, *don't let them kill me. And don't make me kill one of them. Please.*

I began to fill my kitchen sink with warm water. As the water filled, I lifted my daughter's bunny plate and swirled it under the water, soaped it and put it in the dish drainer. One minute had elapsed. They were still out there talking in low voices. I lifted another plate with peanut butter smeared across it, remembering the sandwich I'd made for my son at lunch cut into the shape of a car. I cleaned that, rinsed it thinking the warm water was one of the sweetest things I'd ever felt. They were still out there, mumbling. When I started thinking about the possibilities of what might happen next, I stopped my mind and breathed in the sunlight. The power of the mountains. I looked at a shard of pottery on the windowsill I'd discovered on the land when we first began building. It had a tiny black line crossing it and I tried to imagine what the entire pot looked like before it had been dropped and broken. All I could call up was the image of the clay pigeons I'd blasted with my father. I felt icy and cold as the minutes wore on and they stayed in a circle. My feet were ice-cold numb, I shook and tingled like a tuning fork. I wasn't even sure I *could* run, but my legs were like water. What could they be planning? Surely they would have figured out by now it wasn't me that left in the car with my husband and children; it was another female. They'd been watching the house. This I knew for certain. I washed a glass, once a jelly jar, decorated with seals bouncing balls in bright kindergarten colors. Like a stage set, I knew exactly where important things like my car keys were.

How many steps to get to a window I could bust open with my own weight. I knew I'd run down the arroyo and head for the highway, hiding behind junipers, darting like a rabbit until I got to safety.

I just didn't know where safety was.

I was flooded with more stage dimensions, how many feet made up our kitchen, the length of the entire house kitchen to zome, numbers we'd held in our minds and on our plans for over a year, and now how many minutes it would take to traverse them.

Early building memories flashed and I wondered if this was the way it was before dying, all things flying in front of you in a frantic slide show saying *Remember, remember, remember.*

Meanwhile the thieves seemed to have come to a decision. I don't know how I knew this, but somehow I knew that whatever was coming next, a change was coming.

I turned off the water, trying to figure if I could hold the rifle and manage the car keys at the same time. It was either shoot or run. Fight or flight.

Then I heard the most beautiful sound in the world, footsteps retreating. I ran for my car keys. Pretty soon I heard the trawling sound of their clunker car as it started up, watched the agonizingly slow way they turned in a semicircle before leaving. I saw their dust.

Then I did something I can barely believe, even today. I ran for my car and began to chase them. They were about six car lengths ahead, putting on the speed as they drove down the rutted road. I needed to get closer to get their plate numbers. I prayed for Jerry to show up, but not my family. I was a strange mixture of traumatized and furious. They didn't stop as they pulled onto the main road. They picked up speed. I chased after them trying to memorize their plates. Now I could make out four people in the car. They turned onto the interstate and I followed, but they were swerving from one lane to the next.

As soon as I could, I pulled off the freeway and went to the sheriff's department and ran in. I spurted out the plate numbers, the car description, what had happened. I told them to call Officer Pinot. Everything suddenly looked as if it were happening in slow motion. I shouted at the officer in charge, "Do it NOW." And he did.

I was shaking so badly I felt as if I were experiencing a combination of heart attack and brain seizure at the same time. It took me some time to calm down and I insisted someone drive back with me to my house. An officer stayed close on as we passed familiar sights, the stuffed donkey, the stray cement mixers, the hub caps alongside the road.

Lee was already inside when I got back. I had to retell my horror, but I didn't want to do it in front of the kids, so my sister took them to their room to play with their riding tractor.

I explained what had happened as this new guy took notes. Lee went ashen with the details he took my hands and squeezed them. And when the policeman left we sat down in the zome and I told my sister who looked alarmed, understanding it could have been her, not me, inside the house when they came to call.

Sometime that evening a car drove up. We were at the table. A look shot between us. This time I got closer to the closet, knowing just the sound of a rifle discharging might be enough to keep somebody away. But it was the police. They came in, two of them this time, nodded to all of us, then took over our space, leaned against the sink and told me how lucky I was to be alive.

The felon, Ricardo, had just stabbed his mother in Albuquerque before coming out our way. In addition, there was a kidnap victim in the trunk of his car along with radios, guns, knives and someone else's silver. He was "a mean one," the officer said. "But we got him." He thanked me for the license number and car description.

Apparently, they were caught before they got back to Albuquerque, cuffed and now in jail. In Bernalillo. I wish I could say our troubles ended there. But they didn't. At least I slept well for a few weeks.

I was under a blanket of false security for about three months. During that time our family had suffered badly. First the family home in Mississippi we'd gone to each summer was struck by lightning and burned to the ground in ten minutes. Our friend, Johnny became the bearer of bad news. Lee's folks called Johnny and asked him to relay the information. It was hard to imagine this lovely two-hundred-year-old home filled with Victorian furniture and family mementos going up in smoke. Later when we looked at photographs of the ruin, all that remained were the boxwood hedges that delineated the plantation house, the gathering place for friends and family for literally two centuries.

It was a rugged spring. The dust storms took the word enchanting out of the equation for an accurate description of New Mexico. Although it was warm, it was impossible to be outdoors for long without swallowing dust, getting it in your hair or eyes. Even the children preferred to stay inside.

I had to lay wet towels at all the door thresholds to keep out the dirt. But I ended up dusting the place daily. Still, before dinner the children drew pictures on the tabletop in the grit that had blown in since my last cleaning. I had to string out our clothes in the windows after I washed them as the clothesline was nothing more than a vacuum cleaner for the grit that came, it seemed, all the way from Africa.

It was on such a blustery day Johnny drove up again. This time the news was devastating: Lee's mother had passed away after a year and a half of battling cancer. We were lucky to have seen her one last time at their visit to our home over Easter. As weak as water, she managed to stay lively, though once she fell down on the bricks I'd over polished. The visit was sad, but she was so proud of what we'd achieved, and both parents spoke in glowing terms noticing all the details, the tiles, the chevrons of *vigas*.

Between their visit and the news of her death we'd kept ourselves busy with the plans we were drawing for the last room in our house, now boarded up and nailed down with blankets from a moving company.

It had always been our plan to have this bedroom with its own fireplace and bath, but we'd run out of funds and energy, and moving into the main body of the house became paramount. By drawing, sketching and gathering materials for this expansion, we kept one step ahead of the death we knew was coming.

I remember getting an official document in the mail one day. I tried reading it while down shifting as I drove home. It was a summons to appear as a witness in court and to identify the perpetrator Ricardo Ortiz. My stomach flipped at the thought of being in the courtroom face to face with this guy and his pals who had put me in such a panic that day. That night I fixed myself a Southern tradition for nerves: a bourbon with a Pepto Bismol chaser.

"This is going to be rough."

"I'll be there," Lee reassured me.

"Still, seeing this creep under fluorescent lights make me sick. He'll probably wear polyester pants, maybe even a suit. Slick his hair back. Give me a grin and expose that gap in the front of his mouth."

"You can do it," Lee said, giving me a hand squeeze of confidence.

I wondered how I'd hold up under the pressure. Tried to make a joke.

"What do you call a guy in the Courthouse wearing a three-piece polyester suit?"

"Answer: A felon."

The news of Lee's mother's death sent us into a dither of activity. Finding a sitter to be with the children while we went to New Orleans, shopping, cooking for the time we'd be away. A thousand details flew up.

Time seemed so compressed, I felt I didn't come together until we were en route, a friend driving us to the airport in Albuquerque. I was messing about with the nexus of stuff in my bag when I found the envelope from the court system.

"Jesus. That court date is in three days. We'll be in New Orleans."

"Great. Write him."

"It won't get there in time." I showed him the official stationery. "This is from the District Attorney.

And so we pulled off the freeway, minutes ticking away until plane departure. Lee phoned the District Attorney's office from the highway. He was put on hold. After a few stressful minutes he hung up.

"We'll try again at the airport."

Once we checked in our bags, Lee called again mentioning the name of the defendant.

Immediately the D.A. got on. I watched Lee's face darken as they spoke. I could tell by his tone things weren't going well. And by the way he slammed the phone onto its cradle, I knew something was bad.

"You won't believe."

"What?"

"He said we should write a note of condolence and show up anyway."

"Explain that."

"I know. I said write a letter of condolence to who? Myself? This is my mother and we are going to be at the services. One in New Orleans and one in Mississippi."

"You didn't tell him we were leaving on the next flight, did you? I mean they might send the police to keep us from boarding." I looked around the airport, but all looked calm as passengers wearing bolo ties, women in blue jeans and too much turquoise jostled around.

As the plane lifted, I felt relief. But when I left I didn't know if they'd postpone the court date in order to have me as star witness. The entire time during the funeral these questions made me edgy, unnerved.

New Orleans funerals are exhausting. They are more or less an extension of the city's full throttled intention to look at death square in the face and then offer him a drink. And because our families were long-connected, the lines in the funeral home reminded me of coming out parties, folks chitchatting and hugging, nodding at their friends. In fact one poor man got confused, taking Lee's hand and instead of saying, "I'm sorry," said, "Congratulations."

Then there was the drinking. There was plenty of that before, during and after.

The funeral parlor was over-air conditioned and my hands were frozen as I gripped other hands and nodded as they passed on their condolences. Bourbon was like anti-freeze.

And in Mississippi the drinking got harder.

At last we fell back in exhaustion, finding ourselves being taken to the airport settling on board with dreadful hangovers. I looked at the swamps and wetlands below. The place where I was born, a swamp, a place of wet, soupy extremes. Where we were headed couldn't have been more contrasted. As we flew over Texas, I began to think of what lay ahead and wondered if they'd set the date for the hearing. I needed at least a week to sort out the kind of intense socializing, weeping and partying we'd just crammed into a short four days.

I had that familiar light-headed feeling as we drove home. The altitude from below sea level to 9,000 feet was dizzying. Without the canopy of trees I was confronted with the stark nature of our environment. I passed a familiar sight on the freeway on the way to our home: a gigantic billboard of a cowboy twirling a lasso. The space between his legs was cut out so I could see the hills, arroyos and dots of junipers in the background. The highway was littered with paper, Pampers and one car that appeared to have been totally dismantled alongside the road. Dust storms were still blowing as we drove up. But there it was our handmade home, our children. Nothing else mattered so much.

About a week after we'd returned I saw the familiar sheriff's car trundling down our road, but this time wondered if I might be taken into custody for safekeeping until the trial. It was my old pal Officer Pinot.

"Sorry about that loss," he said respectfully as he entered.

"You understand we had to be at the funeral." I was about to launch into the relationship I had with my in-laws, like first family to me when he stopped me.

"Got some bad news for you."

"What?"

"Ricardo, he escaped. He's out there."

"No."

"Maybe he got to Colorado. We don't know. But if he's around here... "

I knew what he'd say next having to do with self-preservation and firearms. We were back in the dark light of the Wild West.

While we were gone only a number of days, things seemed to have changed in our neighborhood. It was a desperate-feeling season, anyway. My sister and brother-in-law came to visit a few weeks after our return. In frustration at our lack of television, my brother-in-law went out and bought one. Now we were camped indoors with record breaking heat, sometimes as high as 104 degrees, watching the Watergate trials, all of the henchmen answering questions and trying to keep their lies co-coordinated, Nixon sweating under the lights, his secretary performing circus maneuvers to dramatically demonstrate how she'd accidentally erased the important conversations now suddenly a great black hole of memory loss.

The hills were alive with the sound of munching. The plague. Grasshoppers chawed their way across the west, destroying crops, everything in its way. This phenomenon was particularly distressing to those whose smokable cash crop was now making grasshoppers the happiest insect alive. I always wondered if the dope affected the way they jumped. The critters were no laughing matter at the bar. The cross walker, who did odd jobs in the summer while school was out, was given a permanent chair at the end of the bar. He'd fallen into a depression of epic proportions. People drank a lot that summer talking about the plague and watching Nixon on the broken television.

Jerry was at the end of the bar bending a newcomer's ear about how to build with dynamite. This was a spiel I'd heard before.

"Like you never finish a house, man. Finishing it isn't the point. The point is what happens while you build and if you do finish, what's the point? And man, it has to be three dimensional." The guy nodded, but his face read what the f? Jerry went on to describe how a house should be like jewelry. "It's like I'll think about a wall I started a few years back and just go work on that a while. Process, you dig? It's all process."

At this point I leaned over hoping to loosen the lasso Jerry had roped around the stranger's neck.

"Jerry," I said, giving him a small wave. "Ever hear of the Winchester House?"

Jerry looked up, annoyed I'd broken his line of building lore. "No, man."

"It's in California. The widow of the Winchester rifle company lives in it, but believes if she stops building the victims of all the people killed by the rifles will come in and haunt her if she sleeps in the same room twice. So she keeps on building. Driven by ghosts. Dig that."

I read disgust on his crumpled face. I'd out-theoried him.

One night Janis tried to lighten everyone up saying, "well, we don't have to bother to dead head geraniums or marigolds. Grasshoppers doing all the work for us." Nothing seemed to brighten the day. Outside the heat revved up, the grasshoppers kept munching.

During our brief stay in New Orleans we bumped into some old friends who said they "might be coming our way." We were accustomed to folks routed themselves past our house going from East to West. Most of them did show up. But after a few days we could always find work for them to do and their vacation was over. One couple, however, stayed.

It was Edward's fourth wife. At this point in his marital timeline I had no idea how many children he'd dropped onto the planet. Crystal was a mystery, a combination of hippie, healer, actor. She had a way of saying things that made me stop drying dishes and pray for forgiveness. Platitudes such as "I only dig the truth." She was pregnant. And how.

Unlike the small apartment they'd had in New Orleans, our ample space made her feel "free." She felt so free she walked around buck naked wondering why we didn't do that as well.

"Crystal," I said as tactfully as I could, "sometimes the police show up here to give me information about the robbery. I don't know if they'd appreciate your present condition."

"Like they don't like pregnancy?"

"No. They might report me to social services for not taking charge of Lady Godiva exposing herself to my wide-eyed children."

Morgan set to work with his pencils and paper drawing the lump in the middle of her big belly. Lee passed down the hallway glancing at her, trying not to stare and Lilah made her dislike of her nudity clear by throwing pillows in her direction.

"Oh, fuck them," Crystal said stretching out on our sofa, her yoga pose so wide open I could practically see her tonsils from the wrong end. It didn't take long for Crystal to find like-minded friends in the hills, bringing them home where they sprawled on couches and floors. Digging our view.

Finally we had to tell them we weren't a commune. We wanted our privacy. But getting them out was about as difficult as getting our former workers off the property. I thought if I heard her say, "I am an honest person," one more time I might have to turn myself in to the monastery in Las Cruces reserved for crazy priests and nuns.

She started having theatrical events in town. She had an all-nude review I seem to have missed. I was busy on opening night. She called her theatrical production, believe it or not, "Let my people come."

We were now doing finishing touches on the house like grouting tile and re plastering walls the kids had nicked with their cars and trucks. Lee liked to give architectural explanations of our house, explaining where we'd gotten ideas for the door entry and the shapes of the arches. Once he was talking to one of Crystal's friends describing what we wanted to achieve with the three arches in our home.

"The first is Roman." He made a curve in the air. The second was inspired by the Maya." He stopped at the third because it was one of our jump-in-and-do-whatever maneuvers, an arch with no name. Jerry had walked in the back door and down the halls as Lee was explaining the finer points of our home. Since we now had a phone, we became the public pay phone in the neighborhood. Jerry held the receiver up, poised to dial, then said to Lee: "What do you call that last arch? A vagina?"

Jerry had a way of humbling us.

Lee went on. It was long gated, oval shaped with thickened edges.

I still had to make frequent trips to the hardware store for cement and grout. I left Lee to watch the kids while I drove down Fourth Street looking at the damage the insects had caused in the North Valley. The grasshoppers were so thick I had to keep my windows closed as I drove to the highway, lest they jump through the windows. It was sweltering in that car with the windows shut. At least I didn't have to hear about Nixon, just the sound of the wheels on the pavement, the occasional blasts of low-rider cars with horns that blasted a short tune, like the starting bugles at a horse race. I always jumped when one pulled up next to me letting loose with brassy noise.

On the road I was beginning to see some new bumper slogans. Peace signs would always be part of the moving traffic but I noticed some new stickers that signaled a surprising read on the spiritual world. This one stays in my memory: "Beam Me Up Jesus." Was this serious? A new trend? Were we in for the rapture?

As full blown charter members of the food co-op, either Lee or I had to go and lift bags of flour, label bins, the sort of thing that needs doing when a group is run by volunteers. We took turns. Our work gave us good discounts on cheese and honey. I was particularly happy to see the amount of peanut butter I could bring home for so little.

Being a member of the co-op meant you had to bring your own jars. I'd done that in France as well. I remember bringing a milk jug back to the store in Paris that sold dairy products, experiencing deep humiliation as the owner held my bottle up for all the housewives to see. In French she said something like "this is what Americans call clean."

Here, in my hippy co-op I didn't have to suffer like that. Bartering had become a way of life for us. We lived the code of *The Whole Earth Catalog,* the slogan I passed each time I emptied sacks of flour into the bins said it all. Everything was connected to everything.

I was experiencing a sense of relief as I drove home. Even though the heat was devastating, the insects frightening, at least we were in our home. Safe and sound. I thought.

I hauled in the last bag of groceries and kicked the door close behind me so more grasshoppers didn't get inside. But the place was deeply quiet. I found Lee busily working on a tile project.

"Where are the kids?"

"In their room. I guess."

When I went into their room Lilah was quietly reading a picture book. Morgan was on the floor moaning. It looked as if his arm were in four pieces. I nearly fainted.

"Lee. Quick. Morgan's arm. I'm sure it's broken."

I knelt next to him stroking his head. He didn't cry, but closed his eyes in pain.

Lee was horrified to see his broken arm ."I never heard him cry," he explained to me.

We cut up a shoe box to use as a splint then got into the car as fast as we could. Back to the B.C.M.C. emergency room. It took some time to get the X-rays that showed what we already knew. Then he had to have a cast made for his arm. The attending doctor explained that he had to keep it dry and would be changed in a few weeks. He'd done a good job falling off the wall. His arm was broken in three places. "And son, when it heals, it is going to itch."

"How can he scratch it?" I asked. "Knitting needles," he said.

The Jemez mountains were the color of blue corn flour on Morgan's birthday. He'd just had his cast removed so we decided to call the party a cast party, inviting old friends as well as young ones. For party favors I bought squirt guns. About halfway through the event the so-called grownups had a squirt gun fight, ducking behind the mounds of disintegrated adobes, turning the wheel barrow into a place of protection and in general everyone releasing the last of their cabin fever. Jerry showed up, of course, and provided "ammo" for his friends by pouring water from my crystal pitcher which, miraculously, didn't get broken during the event. I remember him in his wool cap, even though it was summer, the sun cutting through the pitcher and refracting light on his plaid shirt. His torso looked like a ballroom on New Year's Eve. Looking back, it seemed that the party was the final hooray for the summer.

Jerry was having so much fun he forgot to get stoned.

Other changes were taking place. From the post office I gleaned lots of folks were talking about leaving, pushing on to Mexico or Costa Rica. Too many Texans moving in, someone said. Land prices going sky high. Turquoise is looking fake, way too blue.

"Developers are coming," one person said.

At the Thunderbird Willy Nelson was singing in his gravelly voice, "Don't Fence Me In," as I went into the only bathroom. All kinds of lewd pictures were scrawled on the stalls with names, phone numbers and what I think was supposed to be a likeness of the women in between the information. The floor was sticky with piss. The sink leaked a brown stain like an old tobacco-chewing dude. And a disintegrating mop stinking of beer, urine and Mr. Clean was propped up in the corner like a truant officer. And Ricardo was still out there. For all I knew he was sitting in a dark corer of the bar watching me with those bullet hole eyes.

That summer, the Watergate scandal kept heating up. We watched Haldeman, Erlichman and Dean sweat it out under the lights of the cameras. These words, conspiracy, cover-up, obstruction of justice droned through our once silent house.

Outside the earth still leapt with grasshoppers, often hitting against the windows like drunken birds in camphor trees.

I remember thinking that the crew-cut coif on the man nicknamed "the brush" was like lawns in the end of summer. I could practically see bugs crawling through his cranium.

I don't know how many times we had to see Rose Mary Woods perform what was dubbed "The Rose Mary Stretch," showing the world how she managed to record over sensitive material. She answered the phone, and hit the record button with her foot, just like the dance we invented at the bar. The so-called "smoking gun tape" phrase was so over-played we used it as a call and response at the bar ending with "obstruction of justice".

At night when it finally cooled down, we'd take walks down in the arroyo and look at a sky free of light pollution. I decided that year sometime in my life I'd take a course in astronomy so I could understand the life span of a star.

We were up early the next day to get into town before the heat pressed down and the wind storms kicked up. Solar showed up at our doorstep.

"What's up," I asked her.

"This is unbelievable, just unfucking believable."

"No. Look at this." She handed me a newspaper. On the front page was a picture of Jerry. He'd been killed in a head-on collision. It was almost beyond comprehension how someone larger than life could no longer be there. He was like the gigantic billboard alongside the freeway, up there with Paul Bunyan.

I got the details of the funeral from Solar. All of his friends at the bar were working on the coffin, embedding turquoise and silver.

Jerry was going out like a pharaoh. I made up a batch of posole to take down to his wife, Dallas. The place was eerie and still, just the sound of the wind in the kite hitting the rafters like a frail bat.

I figured everyone would be working together on the coffin. I looked around at the free form, the weird angles, the stained-glass ceiling, the nails and rebar scattered everywhere. Our work site was less dangerous than their home. But, since they didn't have children, in Jerry's own words I imagined hearing him say, "It's not critical, man."

In a few days word got around that there was going to be a gathering down at the free form for him. I put on my best jeans and a shirt with embroidered flowers. With all the work they'd done on the coffin, they were going to have him cremated. Everything up in flames, like cremations in India. A pyre. Turquoise going back to the earth.

Somehow this burial made sense. It would allow the genie out of the bottle for good.

I found the best shoes I could for the kids. Shoes with closed toes so they wouldn't scrape themselves on the sharp objects that seemed to punctuate the living space in the free form. And then I talked to them both, getting down to knee level so we could have eye contact.

"Listen big. We're just going for a few minutes to pay our respects."

"What does that cost," Lilah asked.

"Pay respects is just a term, like coming to tell them we're sorry

Jerry was killed."

"What did it look like?" Morgan asked.

"Okay, no questions like that. Everybody's a little raw down there. Just imagine the Volkswagen crumpling, crushed with Jerry inside." They looked at each other. "It isn't pretty."

They turned, thinking the lecture was over. "Hold it. Promise me you will not eat anything, drink anything, or get on that roof. And if any kids are there, no running around in the free form. Get far away. There's broken glass everywhere. Besides we won't be there long. Promise?"

Having gotten that out of the way, I sucked in my breath, not even imagining what had been transpiring down there. We could hear loud music as we walked towards the free form.

Jerry really dug the Grateful Dead, so it was fitting that it played out of speakers set next to their ad hoc chicken coop. Thankfully Leroy the killer dog was penned up.

I had a soft moment of remembrance: Jerry strolling down the dirt road, Jon-Jon squawking behind him. From time to time he'd stop and stare at the mountains, then pick up the chicken and stroke it.

Inside the free form folks gathered around tables with cheese and Ritz crackers, dubious looking brownies, watermelon, the third food group for our community, and a punch bowl I stood in front of to make sure the kids didn't partake. Someone had made a dip of mushroom soup and sour cream that tasted awful. And the Vienna sausages wrapped in biscuit dough were burned. Not even a dish of mustard to dip them in to kill the tangy campfire after bite.

Then I noticed a group of the four heavies, as we called Jerry's close friends, digging through a red coffee can. I nodded to the people from the neighborhood as stories lifted and passed throughout the space. Jerry's wife looked dazed. I passed the table with Jerry's model airplanes, the white glue piled up like the last of winter snow. I took her hand and told her how sorry I was. I told her the truth, Jerry was about the most amazing person I'd ever met. Her vacant stare told me she was stoned on something. I went back to my station in front of the food table. Lee walked over to her and said something in a whisper. Again, she didn't seem to know what people were saying.

I decided twenty minutes would be optimum to be there. I didn't have much to say to anyone in the crowd and the false gaiety was making me sad. It reminded me of a hippie version of the funeral we'd attended in New Orleans. Solar showed up and whispered to me that Jerry's old lady was stoned on four hits of acid.

"I figured," I said. I was giving Lee our eye signal to leave when David walked over to me. He showed me the contents of the coffee can. "Like some chicks are going to dig through and find bones. They're going to make weavings with them."

"Macramé is not my thing," I said.

He began rolling a joint, sprinkling some of the contents of the can onto the paper along with dope. He rolled it like the pro he was, took a puff then handed it to me.

"What? Smoke Jerry?"

With smoke in his lungs he could only nod.

"Listen, I really liked the guy, but I refuse to smoke him."

He shrugged his shoulders and began this odd communion. I was first amazed at this gesture, and then I thought how odd it would be to have Jerry banging around in my internal pipes, laughing, smoking and creeping into my head with his strange philosophy.

I tried to warn Lee not to partake, and as I was walking towards him a shadow passed above me. It was Morgan, he'd climbed right onto the stained-glass window. I was about to run, outside and grab him when he crashed right through the glass, landing in front of Dallas. Blood gushed out of the gash in his forehead. It splattered on her like a crime scene.

"Jesus," she shrieked, as if Jerry had fallen to earth in front of her for one last visit. She came apart, screaming and crying. I grabbed Morgan, the cut bleeding profusely, hurried him out, looked for Lilah who had wisely stayed away making mud pies in the barnyard. When she saw Morgan, her mouth formed an O.

Morgan's head wound spurted blood so badly I had to bring three shirts to the emergency room in Albuquerque where he got stitched up. I was reminded of the day I'd gone to the BCMC in labor, been turned away like Mary and Joseph and had to retreat to the drugstore for my remaining hours of labor. The hallways then, and now, were sad and overstuffed with suffering people, residents scurrying around. I heard a nurse talking to another about a gunshot wound, and after a day like we'd just had, I wondered if it was anyone we knew.

I thought I saw the doctor who'd taken care of Morgan's broken arm. We'd been there so recently, I worried they were going to think we were abusing our son It was an odd thought. It had been an odd day.

There was so much turmoil around the accident, papers to fill out at BCMC, and things of that nature, we didn't speak about the "service" until we were on the way home.

"You didn't, you know, smoke any of that stuff, did you?" I asked Lee.

"No. Never know what kind of dynamite they're using."

I told him about the interchange when David offered Jerry's remains. And for some reason, we started laughing. I don't know if it was at the absurdity of life, or relief of tension. But as our car finally chugged up the road, our zome in view, I realized it was warm enough to build again. As we passed the stuffed donkey, I thought, *It's building season, we can finally finish the wing on our house.*